W9-BBU-303

Angels of the Maritimes
By your side

Karen Forrest

Pottersfield Press, Lawrencetown Beach, Nova Scotia, Canada

Copyright © 2008 Karen Forrest

All rights reserved. No part of this publication may be reproduced or used or stored or transmitted in any form or by any means – graphic, electronic or mechanical, including photocopying – or by any information storage or retrieval system, without the prior written permission of the publisher. Any requests for photocopying, recording, taping or information storage and retrieval systems of any part of this book shall be directed in writing to the publisher or to Access Copyright, The Canadian Copyright Licensing Agency, 1 Yonge Street, Suite 800, Toronto, Ontario, Canada, M5E 1E5 (www. accesscopyright.ca). This also applies to classroom use.

Library and Archives Canada Cataloguing in Publication

Forrest, Karen

 Angels of the Maritimes : by your side / Karen Forrest.

ISBN 978-1-895900-99-6

 1. Angels. I. Title.

BL477.F673 2008   202'.15   C2008-900219-9

Cover design by Gail LeBlanc
Cover photos by Lesley Choyce and istockphoto.com
Author photo by Wayne Forrest, W. Forrest Photography

Pottersfield Press acknowledges the financial support of the Government of Canada through the Book Publishing Industry Development Program for our publishing activities. We also acknowledge the ongoing support of the Canada Council for the Arts, which last year invested $20.1 million in writing and publishing throughout Canada. We also thank the Province of Nova Scotia for its support through the Department of Tourism, Culture and Heritage.

Pottersfield Press
83 Leslie Road
East Lawrencetown, Nova Scotia, Canada, B2Z 1P8
Website: www.pottersfieldpress.com
To order phone toll-free 1-800-NIMBUS9 (1-800-646-2879)

Printed in Canada

The Canada Council   Le Conseil des Arts
for the Arts   du Canada

Canadä

NOVA SCOTIA
Tourism, Culture and Heritage

To all the earth angels making this world a more
peaceful place to live.

To the members of the Canadian Armed Forces,
both past and present,
who have served with pride, honour and courage.

Special thanks to my husband, Wayne,
who has always supported and believed in me,
and to my family for standing by my side along my
spiritual journey.

Contents

Prologue

I have written this book in the hopes of helping Maritimers connect with their angels and God.

I sincerely hope you do more than just read this book. My wish is for you to call upon your angels to assist you in your life with everything – big and small. Begin experiencing for yourself the multitude of ways invoking angels will bring joy, love and peace into your life.

If you are seeking a more peaceful, loving and joyful life, then reading these Maritimer angel stories, angel tips and angel messages will inspire you to become just that.

Know that you have guardian angels always by your side guiding you with unconditional love. You are not alone in this world.

Foreword

Karen and I first met in 2005 and since that time I have witnessed her commitment to the wonderful work with Angels that she offers. She has become known to most as "the Angel Lady." Quite fitting that the writing of this book would come at this time, as a gift for those of the Maritimes and beyond.

I have watched on the sidelines as Karen gathered stories and faithfully continued in preparing to bring this book to each of you. Her dedication to Creator/God and the Angels is authentic.

It is a great blessing to share in the joy with those of the angelic realms in the completion of this inspiring book. Angels bring great blessings into our lives and Karen has captured the wonder of this, which will be an inspiration to many. We, of Atlantic Canada, have much to celebrate. Share this wonderful book with friends and family. Their lives will be enriched by it!

May the Angels watch over you, guide and protect you … always.

Noogamijiij (Little Grandmother) Selina WaterEagle
Traditional Medicine Woman
Grandmother's Medicine Lodge, Nova Scotia

Angels Watching Over Us

Hospital Angels

"I was seriously sick in the hospital, feeling afraid and alone. I prayed to Jesus and God to watch over me. Although I tried to keep my spirits up, there were days I felt particularly down, sad and discouraged. However, on these nights, the same doctor would come into my hospital room when I felt my worst, and without speaking, sit on my bed for a few minutes. I would then feel calm and peaceful. Later, when I asked the nursing and hospital staff which doctor was kindly visiting me late at night, no one knew who I was referring to. The nurses informed me they were not aware of any late night visitors in my room. I never saw him again after I left the hospital. It was then that I realized I had an angel visiting and comforting me."

– D.L., Maritimer for Life

Angels are able to take on human form to visit us when we need to feel their loving presence. When you are in the presence of such angels, they speak few, if any, words; they display a strong, peaceful, calming presence, and they only show themselves for a brief period of time. When you are in a time of need, ask your guardian angels to be by your side. Then feel their powerful, loving presence.

Angel Message: "We truly are by your side sending you love and comfort. You never have to go through anything alone in your life. Simply think of us and we are instantly by your side. Keep your heart open to our great love for you."

Saved by an Angel

"Two of my friends and I were going out for the evening dancing. I am married but the other two girls were single. I was voted the designated driver. During our drive we were laughing and joking around trying to decide our lines if anyone tried to pick us up while out dancing. One friend decided to say that she is a transvestite awaiting her final sex operation. My other friend decided to say that she couldn't stay out late because she had a mysterious rash that really bothered her when she started to sweat. We were just trying to think of the silliest things to say.

"I was just pulling out onto the main road when they asked me what I was planning to say to discourage men from trying to pick me up. I was going to use my standard, true and very effective line of 'I'm married with four children,' when I suddenly hit my car brakes in the middle of the intersection and blurted out, 'I can't drive out in front of that truck.' Well, you can only imagine the laughter from the girls from this unexpected sudden stop. I felt a little silly, but I had actually put the car in reverse and allowed a feed truck to pass that was barely in sight when I pulled back in. My mind was persistently telling me, 'I can't be in front of the truck' and something told me not to ignore this particular guidance.

"The truck went on and I pulled out behind it listening to gales of laughter and 'Good one, Mary. I have to remember that one; I am not interested in you because I can't go in front of that truck.' We didn't drive more than two kilometres down the road and the truck collided head-on with a car that had been passing a string of cars and didn't make it. If we had been in front of that truck we would likely have been in the middle of a very deadly accident. One of the women with me that night had just taken a St. John Ambulance first aid course that day. She ran over to help at the accident site, but I intuitively yelled to her, 'It's too late, you can't help the driver.' I had no way of knowing there was only a young man in that car and that he was killed instantly.

"I have no doubt that angels watch over us. I am very grateful I listened to my intuition."

– Mary, Nova Scotia

Have you ever ignored your intuition and then regretted it? Your intuition/gut instincts are your angels and God talking to you. Use your intuition to your advantage in living a fulfilled and safe life.

Always, always trust your intuition and gut instinct, even if it makes no sense at the time. Something was telling Mary to not pull out onto the main road and thankfully she listened to her intuition, even though she didn't know why. Faithfully following her intuition potentially saved Mary's life and the lives of her two friends.

Angel Message: "In trusting your intuition, you are connecting with us, receiving true, divine guidance. By following your guidance, you display faith in how we can lovingly and divinely guide you in every area of your life."

Family Angels Watching Over Us

"Every night I pray for my family's safety and happiness and request the angels to watch over all my family members. One night I felt compelled to individually say each of my family member's names in my prayers. That night I dreamt that I was sleeping by my grandson's crib and I noticed angels and beautiful coloured lights (yet more angels) looking down on my grandson. In my dream, my husband was sleeping in one bedroom and my daughter was sleeping in the next bedroom. Both my husband and daughter had large, white angels watching over them.

"The next morning, when I awoke, I knew with all my heart that my family is constantly protected by angels. I felt warm and comforted knowing there were angels guarding over each of my family members. Per my morning routine, I picked an angel oracle card for my daily angel message. The card I chose was the family card, reassuring me that 'All is well.' Thanks, angels, for watching over my family."

– *H. J., Nova Scotia*

Prayer for Family Protection: Guardian Angels of each and every member of my family, please lovingly watch over us at all times. Surround each and every one of us in your protective wings. Help us feel your powerful love and help us know we are never alone in this world. Thank you, Guardian Angels.

Sentry Angels Watching Over Me

"After I separated from my ex-husband, I was worried about my personal safety. I felt threatened and unsafe as my ex-husband would stalk me and my home.

"Worried for my safety, I called upon the angels to protect me and my home. That day I noticed very tall angels

14

surrounding my house like sentries. They were like warrior angels protecting me and my home! I immediately felt safe and divinely protected. From then on, I no longer worried that my ex-husband would unexpectedly arrive on my doorstep, stalking me. And he never did approach my home again. What a relief to feel safe and sound in my own home."

– A.B., Maritimes

Our homes are meant to be our sanctuaries, to feel at peace and safe in.

Angel Tip: You can ask four guarding angels to always surround your home to keep you and your family safe and protected. In addition, visualize your home surrounded in divine, white light. White light represents divine protection.

Add more angels if you wish. Some people ask for angels at each corner of their house, at each doorway inside the house and outside and at each window. Whatever makes you feel divinely protected. You only need to say this prayer once, but I thank the angels/God on a regular basis for protecting my home. When you have asked for divine protection, please follow your intuition in keeping your home safe. For example, if your gut instinct is telling you to lock your door one day even though you never lock your doors, then lock your doors that day. If something is telling you not to let someone into your home, then pay attention to that 'something is telling me' feeling. The angels guide you, but it is your decision if you wish to listen to this guidance.

Prayer for home protection: Guarding angels, please protect my home, every person in my home, every pet in my home and every object in my home. I ask that four angels surround my home at each corner and one angel to shield my front door. Thank you for your loving protection.

Saving a Soldier

"It was during World War One and I was leaving my hometown in Prince Edward Island to fight in a war overseas. A war that I knew nothing about, but I felt compelled to do my part in serving my country and so I enlisted as a soldier in the Canadian Army. I was only seventeen and did not fully comprehend the stark realities of war. I considered this to be an adventure, a way to make a difference in this world.

"Upon hearing of my enlistment, my classmate Anne, who was fifteen at the time, presented me with a Mother Mary medallion for protection to keep me safe during this horrible war. I was raised in the Catholic Church and I felt and appreciated any protection I could get – including from Mother Mary. I wore this medallion every day to keep me safe and alive while I served overseas. It was a rough time and not easy for me as my fellow soldiers and friends were being injured and killed. But it was not my time to die.

"At war's end (the war to end all wars!), I arrived home in Prince Edward Island, very grateful to be alive. I showed my family my Mother Mary medallion that I had worn without fail, every day I was overseas during the war. There was a dent in the medallion where a bullet had hit me. If it weren't for this medallion, I would have been killed. The bullet hit the medallion directly, thus saving my life! Thank you, Mother Mary, for looking out for me."

– Bill (as told by his family),
Prince Edward Island

Along with angels and God, there are of course very loving, powerful ascended masters, such as Mother Mary, to call upon in your life. It does not matter what your religious or spiritual beliefs are. You are welcome to call upon any ascended master, such as Mother Mary, Jesus, Buddha, or Moses, to guide you in your life. Many of them come from various religions and cultures, yet they are nondenominational for anyone can call upon them. Ascended masters are great spiritual healers and teachers who have once lived upon this earth. They do not differentiate based on your religious beliefs. They will lovingly help anyone who asks. Yet more divine beings by your side!

Note: As a medium, able to communicate with deceased people, I called upon Bill to see what messages he had for us. Here is Bill's message: "Never leave out God in your life, for doing so means you leave out love. Without love for each other we are at war. Live in respect and harmony. Honour each other, even if you don't understand each other. You are capable of living in harmony. The choice is yours. May you never live in the state of war that I lived through. My fellow comrades who died in war, died to bring you peace. Now live in peace. May no one else ever die in the name of war."

Maritimer Angels:
Faithfully By Your Side

A Coat for Sarah

"I only had one child, and I wanted to do my best in providing for her. Winter was just around the corner and my ten-year-old daughter, Sarah, needed a new winter coat. I was determined to purchase Sarah a new coat for school. As money was extremely tight, I was completely relying on my faith in God for this to happen.

"Sarah and I picked out a pretty, blue, warm coat from a large department store and had it set aside for lay-away. Each week I prayed to God to help my husband and me make the payments for Sarah's coat. Each week, we managed to come up with the money. One week, we simply had no money to make the payment on Sarah's coat and winter was fast approaching. I prayed even more and completely believed God would provide for us – even if I didn't know how. That week, I received a letter from the department store stating the final payments were made on the coat and the coat was now paid in full! I very thankfully and joyfully picked up Sarah's coat just as the winter season was

upon us. I believe in small miracles. I remain firm that my family's needs shall be taken care of as I continue to have unwavering faith in God and my angels."
— *Bessie MacKinnon, Prince Edward Island*

Your angels do not want you to lack for anything in your life. Never hesitate to express your needs. You can think them, say them, write them out or pray for your needs. Have faith your prayers will be answered. Be specific when asking for what you need. For example, ask for a four-bedroom house with a garage versus a nice house or a pay increase of ten percent versus a pay increase. Do not micromanage God and your angels by telling them how you want something achieved as you only limit them by doing so. Your angels are much more creative in bringing things about than you can ever imagine. Release the "how's" and instead focus on following your intuition, which is your angelic guidance.

Prayer to release the "how's": Angels and God, I completely release the 'how this will happen' to your divine infinite wisdom. I release control, worry and fear surrounding the 'how' things should happen. I simply affirm that it will happen and let it be. Thank you for graciously meeting all of my needs.

Hotel Reservations: Angel Style

The following is my personal example of how I asked specifically for something in my life, just to make my life a bit easier that day.

I was attending my Professional Teachers Spiritual Training workshop by Doreen Virtue in Laguna Beach, California. This was my third trip to Laguna Beach for certification by Doreen Virtue and I remembered my hotels being rather expensive my last two trips. This time I was smart enough to call upon my angels to assist me in finding a cheaper hotel. I asked my angels, 'My guardian angels, please help me find a cheaper hotel room (under $150 per night), within a fifteen-minute walk of where the workshop is taking place, a three-star hotel or better, clean, non-smoking room, with a queen- or king-size bed, and with availability for the dates I need. Thank you, angels.' Now that is being specific!

I had absolute faith that my angels would help me find the perfect hotel. I checked out some hotels on the Web and some hotel brochures. That day, I booked myself into a three-star hotel, for only $89 per night, a non-smoking room with a king-size bed and only a ten-minute walk from the workshop I was attending. The bonus was that it was a beachfront hotel with a swimming pool.

Faithfully Fixing My Car

"I had just received the devastating news that my father had passed away. I was married with three young girls and grieving the death of my father. At the time I was living in Halifax, Nova Scotia, where my husband was posted with the Canadian Navy. By pure coincidence, or Divine timing, my husband had just returned two days previously from be-ing at sea for three months.

"For convenience, my husband and I decided to drive to Prince Edward Island for my father's funeral rather than fly. We needed the car to get around the island. Only thing was our car was old and in the past couple of days we had heard a funny sound coming from the car's engine.

"My husband, Ron, decided to take our car to the me-chanic first before attempting the four-hour drive to Prince Edward Island. While my husband was talking to the me-chanic, I sat nearby and prayed that our car would be fixed without any repairs. We just didn't need the extra expense of car repairs and we needed to drive to Prince Edward Island that day to assist with funeral arrangements. We did not have time to spare.

"The mechanic test drove our car, carefully listening for this funny noise, but could hear nothing. The mechanic looked at my husband in confusion as the car was running completely fine. My husband confidently exclaimed, 'Oh don't worry about it. My wife was praying for the car to be fixed, so I have no doubts it is fixed now!'

"I had complete faith the angels would fix our car and they did. We had a safe trip to Prince Edward Island and our car never did make that funny noise again!"

– *Fran Doucette, Prince Edward Island*

Have you ever lacked faith in your life? Most people have at some point in their lives. The important thing to remember is that you can ask God and your angels to increase your faith.

Prayer for increased faith: God and my angels, I do believe in you, but sometimes need to know that you are there for me. Please increase my faith in you. Remind me that together we can accomplish anything. Thank you.

Touched By An Angel

An Angel's Loving Touch

"At the tender age of fifteen, I had endured a traumatic experience in my life. As I was leaving the police station, my tears would not stop flowing. I felt distraught. However, I had to get onto the bus alone and take a forty-five minute journey into the city to meet with a psychologist, at the IWK hospital. While sitting quietly on the bus, I suddenly felt a warm loving hand on my shoulder. When I turned around to see who was offering her hand in comfort, I realized that there was no one sitting around me! Then as I glanced out the bus window, I observed a beautiful reflection of a blond-haired woman smiling at me and I suddenly felt deeply comforted. I realized seconds later that she did not really exist. I started to question my imagination, but deep down I wondered if I had seen an angel reaching out to me in comfort and love.

"My second angel encounter occurred a month later. I was still grappling to overcome a very difficult time in my life. As I sat in church praying for help, I looked up and saw a beautiful angel who was close to the church's ceiling.

She was very large, wore a beautiful white opalescent gown and was smiling directly at me. At first I thought I was seeing things so I looked over at my mother sitting beside me to see if she noticed this angel. My mother appeared oblivious to my vision as she continued to pay attention to the service. Then I started to question my sanity. How come my mother wasn't noticing this angel? Why wasn't anyone else in the church looking up in awe as I was? Do people really see angels? But deep within my heart, I knew I was seeing an angel. After all, I had just been praying for divine help! With this angel's presence, I felt at peace. While looking at this beautiful, smiling angel, I absolutely knew everything would be taken care of. I was going to be just fine."

– *Natalie, Nova Scotia*

Your angels want to connect with you and for you to feel their unwavering love. Never hesitate to ask your angels for comfort, love, and peace of mind when going through a rough time in your life as this is one role of your guardian angels. Sometimes you may feel their presence, as if an angel hugged you or touched you on your shoulder or cheek. You may see an image of an angel, as Natalie described, or someone will give you a picture of an angel or an angel pin. You might hear loving words, almost as though you are talking to yourself, but you are not making it up, or you may experience a sense of knowingness that you are surrounded by angels by your side.

Needing angelic/divine presence in your life? Then simply pray or ask or think: "Angels/God, I need to know that you are truly with me. Please help me feel your presence and help me see you. Open my heart to you. I thank you for always being by my side."

Angel Message: "Dear ones, draw on our strength and love for you. We are always by your side. Our love for you is unconditional. Simply ask us/think about us and we are right there ready to infuse our precious love for you into your hearts. Call upon us frequently so that you may know and feel our love."

Hearing God's Love

"I was practising on increasing my clairaudient capabilities (the ability to hear angels/God) and I often practised on my bus ride home from work each day. (Anything to pass the time on a city bus ride!)

"One afternoon, I was yet again asking my guardian angels and God to offer me a message by my hearing them directly. I relaxed my mind and remained open to this. (This was all so new to me!) As I continued to relax and breathe, I suddenly heard a loving voice from inside me proclaim, 'My holy child, you are loved.' I knew intuitively that this loving message was from God. The voice was a low, strong, sure-sounding voice. I intuitively knew it was not me talking to myself. I was very grateful (and surprised) to receive this divine message! It renewed my faith in communicating with angels and God."

– Anonymous Maritimer

There are various ways angels communicate with you. Hearing them, or clairaudience, is one way. All messages from your angels and God are given in loving, positive words. Angels never communicate in a negative way. Angels would never tell you that you are stupid or don't know what you are doing. Angels communicate in an uplifting manner to lovingly guide you on your life path and life's purpose. Angels and God often address you as holy child, beloved child, dear one or other endearing terms. This is a sign you are communicating with angels and not talking to yourself. (Have you ever talked to yourself, beginning with the words "beloved one"?) Also, when communicating with you, angels/God say "we" versus "I." When you hear the word "I" that is an indication of you talking to yourself versus Divine communication. When you hear the word "we" that is a definite indication you are communicating with angels/God.

Angel Message: "We always speak to you in loving terms, such as you deserve. We love you completely and would never speak in a negative way, for how would that encourage you on your life's path? Listen to your inner voice that speaks in a loving, repetitive, positive way. That is us talking to you!"

Seatbelt Reminder

"We live in a small town in Nova Scotia and when I am just going on a short drive to the store or bank I almost always forget to put my seatbelt on. When my wife is with me, before even leaving our driveway, she does not hesitate to remind me to wear my seatbelt. However, when she isn't with me there is a good chance I will forget.

"While my wife was working, I decided to do some Christmas shopping by myself. I quickly finished my shopping and started to pull out of the store parking lot, when I felt a gentle tap, like a wing tip, on my left shoulder. I turned to see what had tapped me and there was the seatbelt staring me in the face. I could just imagine my wife firmly saying, 'Don't forget your seatbelt.' So I immediately put my seatbelt on and drove home. When I arrived home and my wife asked me why I was grinning, I told her that my angels had reminded me to put on my seatbelt; however, they were a lot quieter at it than she was."

– *Newman Purchase, Kingston, Nova Scotia*

Many people are clairsentient, which means they can literally feel an angel's presence. Like Newman, people commonly feel an angel tenderly tapping them on their shoulder to capture their attention, along with a sudden feeling of comfort, love or protectiveness. At first you look around wondering who tapped you on the shoulder and yet you visually see nobody. This is an indication it is your guardian angel trying to get your attention. It is usually a subtle touch that you may doubt even occurred. But trust this guiding angel touch for it is definitely real.

Angel Message: "It is common for us to lovingly touch you on your shoulder to receive your attention. We truly desire to keep you safe on your journeys and carefully watch over you while you drive."

Archangel Michael: By Your Side

Angel Name Tags

"My family and I had just moved to Spain and were still unfamiliar with the area and language when my young son became seriously ill. He had appendicitis and needed immediate surgery. As I was driving him to the hospital, we pulled into the gas station to fill the car up. I was desperately trying to steady my nerves. Here I am away from my native Canada and I was becoming very anxious, worrying about my son's health. I needed a sign that things were going to be all right and I prayed for my son.

"I have never been the most adventurous driver and was terrified of the idea of driving into this foreign city with its one-way streets and narrow cobbled streets with only a hand-drawn map guiding me. As we waited for the attendant to pump the gas, I looked over at my son and reassured him, 'It's okay, honey, we'll just ask our angels to help and you are going to be okay.' He looked over at me with a wide grin and exclaimed, 'Mom, I don't think I'm the one who needs an angel.' We laughed at that and it lightened the mood a little. Just then, I looked over at the name tag of the gas attendant and couldn't believe my eyes. His name tag read 'Angel Michael.' I kid you not. I offer you this story as we all need to know that we are not alone, ever."

– Lisa-Marie Deveau, Moncton, New Brunswick

Archangel Michael protects, gives you courage, helps you with your life purpose, and fixes things. He is associated with both Judeo-Christian and Islamic religions; however, regardless of your religious/spiritual beliefs you can call upon Archangel Michael. He is also considered the patron saint for military members and police officers. When I served a six-month tour in Bosnia as a military nurse, rest assured I called upon Archangel Michael to be by my side and keep me safe.

Angels will provide you with messages clairvoyantly: that is, through your psychic vision. In this instance, Archangel Michael chose a physical sign to catch Lisa's attention and remind her that she is not alone and he is there to protect Lisa and ensure her child is safe. Keep your eye out for signs from angels, letting you know they are by your side. Angels can manipulate real life objects such as the name tag to grab your attention. It was no doubt a huge relief to Lisa to see Angel Michael's name.

Archangel Michael's Protective Force

"On September 30th, 2003, Hurricane Juan had Nova Scotia in its destructive path. It made land at Halifax/Dartmouth with widespread damage and devastation. The noise made by the wind was unlike anything I had ever heard before – like a train would sound if you were standing beside the track as it passed by at top speed but relentless and for hours, all night long. For the first time in my life, I was truly afraid during a storm! The power had gone off hours earlier. My husband and I were in total darkness. Even with candles lit, it was impossible to settle down and relax. The noise was horrendous and there was no question we were in the middle of a hurricane.

"I had recently read some books about angels and was trying out some of the lessons suggested by these books. I prayed for God to send Archangel Michael to protect us through this storm and to post angels at the four corners of our townhouse unit to stand guard through the night and keep us safe. I thanked the angels for their powerful presence. Only then was I able to relax enough to finally sleep. I felt a sense of peace, even though the storm still raged outside.

"In the morning, all was quiet. The devastation outside was heartbreaking. We ventured outside to assess the damage. Our neighbours on both sides had been up all night bailing water that had come in through their front windows and doors. They had numerous shingles missing and one unit next to me had lost all the siding off the side of the home. We had no damage whatsoever to our unit. Even our old window, original to the house and next to be replaced on our never-ending to do list, had not leaked. These same windows had leaked in other storms. Our only damage was to a large, old maple tree at the back of our yard. Two of the maple's big branches broke and crushed the back fence. The grass in the backyard had so many trees down we could actually see the lake beyond them. None of these broken, uprooted trees had fallen towards us, as experienced by some of our neighbours.

"A state of emergency was declared for our Maritime region. Our power was out for a week. Crews from outside of the province came to help clear away the fallen trees and debris, but were unable to clean up our greenbelt until the following year.

"My faith in angels is unwavering. I had all the confirmation I needed. There is rarely a day goes by that I don't enlist their help and Archangel Michael is always one I call upon.

"I often wonder if I had extended my request of protection to include the four corners of the property and not just my house if our beautiful maple tree would have remained undamaged. But I am immensely grateful for the powerful protection I had for my family and home."

– Donna MacInnes, Dartmouth, Nova Scotia

Archangel Michael's message: "Never hesitate to call upon us. We are here to keep you safe and protected. Simply say/think our name and we are instantly by your side. Yes, you can send us to protect and watch over others too! It is our honour to lovingly guard over you. You are safe in our loving hands."

Fixing Angels for Toilets

Here is one of my personal favourite examples when I called upon Archangel Michael to help me fix something.

I was attempting to replace a toilet seat for the first time in my life (I am not exactly known for being a handywoman around the house). I was determined to do this small task on my own since my husband was away and couldn't help me. I called upon Archangel Michael known for helping to fix things and the angels of fixing toilets to assist me.

I started off well, but quickly became stuck trying to remove the second screw on the old toilet seat. My first reaction was impatience. I wanted this ugly, old toilet seat removed and I needed it done quickly as I had to leave for work soon. So I took a quick break, sat down on my living room couch and talked to the angels. 'I still really need your help. For some reason, I can't unscrew this one screw. Please help me. I don't want to ask for human help. Please don't embarrass me by making me ask for help when half my toilet seat is off.'

After sitting for one minute, calmly breathing in and out deeply, I went back to my toilet seat replacing. Suddenly, I distinctly heard the angels instruct me, 'Use the clamp in the other direction. You are screwing it off in the wrong direction.' I was accidentally tightening the screw on instead of loosening the screw off! I followed the angels' guidance and successfully replaced my old toilet seat with a fancier, sea-patterned one.

Angel tip: To better connect with your angels in listening to their guidance, take deep breaths in and out. Deep breathing physiologically relaxes your body, which opens you up spiritually. When you breathe shallowly, this blocks spiritual guidance. Guidance and healing is received on your in breath and releasement takes place with your out breath. Pay attention to and follow the guidance you intuitively receive. You cannot effectively receive divine guidance if you are holding your breath or breathing shallowly. Breathe, just breathe!

Blessing My Car

"My transmission went on my van. The estimate to fix it was over $3,000! Being mechanically inclined and having an educational background in mechanics, I decided to try and fix the transmission myself – a first for me. I called upon angels and God to help me fix my van's transmission. My wife called upon Archangel Michael to assist, as she had learned that Archangel Michael is the archangel of fixing things. I had the whole transmission laid out on my basement floor. Determinedly, I looked up information on the Internet to assist me with instructions on replacing my transmission. I ordered the parts for only $250 – big savings from the quoted $3,000. Over a period of a few days, I successfully pieced together my van's transmission. Just before placing the transmission into my family van, I blessed the transmission with holy water. Before turning the key to start the van, I again called upon the angels to assist me and immediately the van started up smoothly!"

– Wayne Murnaghan, Prince Edward Island

To call upon Archangel Michael to help fix something, think, pray or say aloud, "Archangel Michael, I ask for your assistance and clear guidance in fixing (name the item or task). Thank you for your help." Then intuitively trust what comes to you for guidance.

Angel Tip: If you rely on a mechanic or someone else to fix your vehicle, call upon Archangel Michael to guide your mechanic to quickly, easily and cheaply fix your vehicle.

Working Courage

"Have you ever dealt with a rude co-worker or boss that drives you crazy? This was my workplace dilemma. As an administrative assistant, I work in a very busy office with three other administrative assistants. I love what I do and get along with my co-workers, but admittedly I have a strained relationship with my direct supervisor. I considered her style to be abrupt in manner and at times disrespectful with her comments.

"One day she appeared to be stressed and consequently snapped at me, 'What took you so long to have these papers ready to be sent out?' This sarcastic comment was not appreciated considering I was busy answering the telephone the past hour. I felt like snapping back a rude comment, but this wasn't like me. I was taught to be respectful towards others and act politely. I was determined not to stoop to my supervisor's level.

"That day I left work still stewing over my supervisor's rudeness and general lack of appreciation. I was tired of her snide remarks. I wanted the courage to stand up for myself in a respectful way by informing my supervisor I was no longer going to tolerate her rudeness.

"I believe in angels and had recently taken a workshop on archangels where I remembered learning that Archangel Michael worked with courage. That evening I sat down in my old, comfortable armchair and mentally called upon Archangel Michael. I asked him to give me the courage to stand up for myself and actually say something to my supervisor. I don't like drawing attention to myself as I am a rather quiet person, so I really needed to draw upon Archangel Michael's strength. I remember telling him, 'Archangel Michael, please give me the courage to stand up for myself. I am tired of my supervisor's snide, rude comments. Give me the courage to say something to her. Please help me resolve this in a harmonious manner and also help me believe this issue can actually be resolved. I ask for inner courage and strength. Thank you, Archangel Michael.'

"The next day, before leaving for work, I once again asked Archangel Michael for lots of personal courage. The morning went smoothly, but just after lunch, as I was typing up a letter, my supervisor handed me a package and sarcastically asked, 'Do you think you can get this out on time for the mail pick-up today?' I was sick and tired of this sarcasm. I mentally called upon Archangel Michael, took a deep breath and simply replied, 'I don't appreciate your sarcasm. Please drop the sarcasm because I no longer want to hear it. Just simply let me know what you need me to do.' As I was saying this, I swear I felt the strength of Archangel Michael right beside me. I was shocked, yet very relieved that I stood up to my supervisor. She, in turn, appeared startled, but surprisingly commented no further.

My supervisor placed the package on my desk and quickly walked away.

"For the next two weeks straight, I continued to call upon Archangel Michael to provide me with the courage to stand up for myself and improve my working relationship with my supervisor. Two more times I asked her not to be rude to me and each time I felt more confident in myself to speak up. I noticed that my supervisor was miraculously acting more polite, not only to me, but also to my other co-workers. Thank you, Archangel Michael, for not only giving me the courage to stand up for myself, but also increasing the workplace harmony.

"I learned that I had more inner strength and courage than I ever realized and I'm no longer afraid to use it."

– Maritimer at Heart

Like the above woman, I have countless times asked Archangel Michael to infuse me with inner courage to make changes in my life. If you ever feel a need for inner courage for any situation, then mentally call upon Archangel Michael to aid you. Simply think: "Archangel Michael, please infuse me with inner courage. Give me the strength and courage I need to do (state your situation)." Then quietly sit still for a few minutes and deeply breathe in courage and breathe out any fears, worries or concerns. Feel yourself being engulfed with deep inner courage. Become comfortable with feeling this courage. Feel Archangel Michael's powerful presence surrounding you. Remember that deep breathing is an important part of healing and working with angels. As you breathe in you heal; as you breathe out, you release.

Maritimer Pets: By Our Side

Pet Heaven for Smokey

"Smokey, my beautiful grey half Siamese cat, and I were lounging on the bed watching a show concerning 'Is there a Heaven?'. The host was speaking with the insightful Dalai Lama, inquiring if animals also transition to heaven. The Holy Dalai Lama declared he believed this to be true. He also believed that animals could reincarnate into higher forms if they were good in this life. I turned to Smokey and encouragingly joked, 'See, kitty, if you are a good boy, you can reincarnate!' With that, Smokey took a long look at me, crawled into his bed, and instantly took a heart attack and was passed on in five minutes!

The night that he died I used my deck of angel cards (Messages From Your Angels by Doreen Virtue) and asked Smokey to send me a message. The angel card that turned up was 'Your loved ones in Heaven are okay and happy!' Wow! I know within my heart that my precious cat Smokey is happy on the Other Side."

– Paula, Nova Scotia

As a certified medium, I often have people inquire if their deceased pets also go to heaven. Our deceased pets, along with our deceased loved ones, do cross over to an afterlife – our pets have souls, as do human beings, that continue on in the afterlife. Rest assured, your pets are happy and loved in the afterlife.

Angel Message: "Please know we love all creatures, animals and of course your human pets. We gently watch over them in the afterlife. We surround your pets with our unconditional love. They, like your human relatives, are at peace."

Heavenly Sign From Normy

I am a cat lover and one day I desperately needed a team of divine beings by my side. Following is my personal tribute to my cat Normy.

My precious cat Normy was nineteen years old and needless to say her health was deteriorating. My husband and I are both cat people, so no surprise that Normy was treated like a family member – a royal family member at that. Her nickname was Little Princess. I remember first bringing Normy into our home. She was a beautiful black cat with white toes and white belly and I loved her long hair. I kept a close eye on her health, knowing that I would eventually have to make a decision about euthanizing Normy for I did not want her to suffer needlessly. She was deaf, arthritic and suffered from dementia.

Unfortunately, this day came all too soon. Normy's health was deteriorating quickly; she was losing even more weight and could barely eat. It was with a heavy heart that I took Normy to the veterinarian to be put to sleep. This was heartbreaking for me. When I walked into the veterinarian's office, the staff knew immediately who I was as

I arrived with tears pouring down my face and unable to talk. I was immediately escorted into a quiet room with Normy. I knew I needed to pull myself together so that I could focus on Normy; therefore, I called upon extra angels of comfort to be with me. I immediately felt a sense of comfort spread throughout me. I knew I was doing the right thing for Normy, regardless of how hard it was for me.

I then silently called upon extra fairies, the guardian angels of pets, to surround Normy. Then I called upon God, Archangel Azrael and one thousand extra angels to surround Normy and guide her in the afterlife. I noticed that Normy immediately appeared at ease and comfortable, even though earlier she acted agitated. I was so immensely grateful for the fairies, angels and God's help during this difficult time.

Before Normy was euthanized, I thanked her for being my precious, loving cat and for being in my life. I asked her to give me a sign after she had crossed over to let me know that she was doing well in the afterlife. Two days later, while I was busy with paperwork in my office, I suddenly had an image flash in my mind of Jesus holding Normy in his arms. Jesus was smiling at me and Normy looked healthier and more peaceful than I have ever seen her. I felt a sense of peace permeate my body. I knew without a doubt that this was a sign from Normy letting me know that she was just fine.

If you are mourning the death of your beloved pet, silently ask your pet to give you a sign that they are fine. A sign may come as a sudden visual image, such as I received. You may feel your pet around you, brushing up against you or feel them curled up on your bed. You may have a vivid dream about your pet. Maybe a particular happy memory of your pet will suddenly come to you when you weren't even thinking of your pet. All are signs that your pet is at peace in heaven.

Sammy Earned His Wings

"On a cold spring morning, my son Aaron walked out the back door of our home, not realizing that our budgie Sammy was out of his cage, flying around the house. We often let Sammy out of his bird cage for his shower. He loves to take it in our kitchen sink by running through the stream of water from the faucet.

"In no time Sammy had escaped the house. Before we realized it, Sammy flew out the back door in a heartbeat, so high that it was only a matter of seconds before we were no longer able to see him.

"We searched up and down our road hoping that he would come to us as we desperately called his name, but he never returned, despite our constant calling. So I decided to write an ad and post it at our local grocery store in hopes that maybe someone would find Sammy or see him around our community. Far-fetched I know, as budgies have no homing sense. But having great faith, we prayed every day and night for Sammy to return home.

"Over the next few nights, it was very chilly and rainy, so our expectations of Sammy ever surviving the weather, not to mention predators, were very slim. Then it happened ... Late Tuesday afternoon I received an unexpected phone call. It was a neighbour approximately one quarter mile away saying that they had found Sammy. While their little girl was playing outside she was startled, as Sammy flew down from a tree and landed on her head. So Aaron and I left to go to their home immediately to bring Sammy back home. When we arrived, the mother of the little girl said that her husband took one of the phone number tabs off my ad and threw it up in their cupboard 'just in case.' After giving the little girl a much deserved reward, we took Sammy home for a much needed recuperation. What an immense relief to have Sammy back safe and sound.

"The following day, I went to the local grocery store to remove the ad and guess what? There was only one phone number taken off the ad. Coincidence? That's not all. The children's names living in the home where Sammy landed were Robin, Wren and Jay.

"Sammy is surely our little miracle."

– Anita Russell Baker, Jeddore, Nova Scotia

Prayer for Finding a Lost Pet: Call upon Archangel Raphael to help you find your lost pet.

"Archangel Raphael, please watch over our beloved pet (name). Guide our beloved pet back home quickly and safely as we miss him/her dearly and desire (name) back home right away. Thank you!"

Raphael is an archangel of Judaism, Christianity and Islam; however, anyone, regardless of their religious or spiritual beliefs, can call upon Archangel Raphael. Raphael is a powerful healer and his name means "God has healed," based upon the Hebrew word *rapha*, which means "healer."

Maritimer Fairies: By Your Side

Merlin and the Fairies

"I have a beautiful Persian cat named Merlin who is almost three years old. As he developed from a kitten to an adult cat, his lower jaw twisted, which made eating difficult for Merlin but he learned to manage and compensate. He has always eaten dry food.

"I brought Merlin to the vet in May 2007 to have his mouth checked. His gums were very red and inflamed, his teeth were very brown, his breath was extremely bad and he wasn't eating very much. Not the healthy condition I preferred my prized cat to be in! My vet informed me that Merlin had severe gingivitis caused by his deformed jaw and the only way to fix it was surgery. The vet placed my cat under anesthesia and scraped his teeth and under his gums, which is very painful but the alternative of Merlin losing his teeth and having continuous infections sounded worse.

"I had just finished reading *Healing with the Fairies* by Doreen Virtue so I decided to ask the fairies for help. I would do pretty much anything to help my cat remain healthy. I explained to the fairies Merlin's health problem and what would happen if his mouth didn't get any better and asked if they would help.

"A few days later, I noticed Merlin was eating more, so I looked in his mouth and although I didn't see much of a difference in his gums and teeth, his breath wasn't as bad. Slowly over the weeks, his mouth has improved tremendously with him having only one or two spots where the gingivitis was really bad. His teeth are just a little yellow now, the bad breath is gone and he is running around playing again.

"I am not sure what I am going to tell the vet when I take Merlin back for his check up and she asks how his mouth healed so well. I will leave that to the fairies. I am not sure what Merlin would have had to go through if I hadn't asked for the fairies' help, but I am extremely grateful to them every day for their help and the happiness and joy they have brought into all of our lives."

– Carolyn Purchase,
The Mystic Meadow,
Berwick, Nova Scotia

Just as we have guardian angels, so do our pets. Fairies are the guardian angels for our pets. Every living pet and animal has a fairy constantly by their side. One of the fairies' roles is to lovingly care for and protect animals and pets. If you are concerned about your pet's health or behaviour, call upon the fairies to assist you. Fairies love working with animals and willingly help people who love their pets.

To ask the fairies for assistance, pray, "Fairies, please help me heal my pet (pet's name). Heal him/her completely, quickly and fully. Guide me in what I need to do to help my pet. Thank you for your healing powers."

Sparkling Fairies at Work

"One night just before falling asleep, I was saying my good night prayers. I was in bed and suddenly viewed some beautiful small lights. Some of these lights were bright white, some blue coloured, some were flashing lights that moved quickly all over the place in front of me. I intuitively knew these were angel lights and fairy lights from recently reading a book on angels. I remember saying to myself how beautiful these lights were. But I really wanted to see these sparkling lights during the daytime to reassure myself they were real and not my imagination. I appreciated the fairies' efforts in showing themselves to me, as I was recently learning to connect with the fairies. Not wanting to ignore them, I simply asked the fairies to show themselves to me during the day when I was wide awake.

"A few days later, I was at work standing by the printer when I looked up and saw beautiful, tiny lights of various colours sparkling above me! The fairies decided to appear to me at my workplace. I quickly looked around to see if any of my co-workers were noticing these beautiful sparkling fairy lights, but no one else appeared to have noticed or at least weren't admitting to it! Thank you, fairies, for brightening my day at work!"

– Rhonda, Nova Scotia

Fairies can be seen visually as tiny, colourful sparkling lights that move about quickly, like a firefly. Of course, fairies can also be observed as you expect a fairy to look – small bodies with delicate butterfly or dragonfly type wings.

Fairy Tip: If you would like to visually see a fairy then simply hold the intent, "Fairies, please show yourselves to me clearly so that I may recognize you and feel your presence. Thank you for your joyful presence." Do not force this to happen. Simply ask and let it happen when the fairies are ready to appear. Do not hold your breath – this prevents you from seeing the fairies. Keep practising and trust when the fairies appear to you.

Fairy Rewards

"I love to walk outside for exercise and to connect with the fairies' joyful energy. Almost always, when walking, the fairies guide me to pick up garbage off the ground. So much so, that I now always carry plastic bags to throw the garbage in while I am walking outside.

"One day, in early spring, I was walking around the lake beside my home. The fairies had me out there for thirty minutes picking up garbage that had accumulated over the winter months. I couldn't pick any more that day as I had to start my workday. I promised the fairies I would come back to this lake within a few days and that this time I would commit to picking up garbage for one hour. Now it turned out, the day I made this promise was Earth Day, a perfect day to commit one hour of my time to help clean the earth!

"Three days later, I did go back as I promised the fairies for I did not want to break my promise (even to fairies, which I know not everyone believes in, but I do!). It was easy to make the promise at the time, harder to accomplish later. While picking up the garbage, I was certainly feeling this in my legs and getting quite a physical workout. Nothing like doing two things at once – cleaning up the earth and working out at the same time.

At one point, I was beginning to curse the people who carelessly littered, but then realized I could put my thoughts to better use. Remembering that the fairies are great manifesters, I asked the fairies if they could reward me for all my garbage picking. Even if I found a quarter, I would be happy. Minutes later, while still picking up garbage, I found a Tim Hortons Roll up the Rim to Win® with 'coffee' written on it and then five minutes later I found another winning tab for a donut. Coffee and a donut was my grateful reward for picking up so much garbage! What was a surprise was that both these winning tabs were already carefully ripped away from the cups – I had not found the coffee cups. Thanks, fairies!"

– K.D., Good Old Maritimer

Cleaning Up the Neighbourhood

"I'm an environmental biologist by trade and nothing irritates me more than looking out my window and seeing tons of garbage on the ground. I had just bought a commercially zoned house, and every time I looked outside on the empty lot next door, which was essentially the only backyard I had, my blood boiled over with rage day after day. Wrappers, coffee cups, shopping bags, takeout containers, newspapers, you name it, and it was there littered on the ground.

"One day, I had no clients so I finally ventured outside with unmatching Rubbermaid gloves and a box of garbage bags. It was time for me to stop grumbling about the litter and do something about it. As far as I was concerned, the issue had finally become urgent, and I knew that the reward of looking at a nice clean lot each time I had a spare minute would be a reward in itself. The lot next door, by the way, was for sale for $1.5 million, so I was a little annoyed that the owners didn't consider picking up garbage and weren't considering the impact on the sale of this property.

"After ninety minutes of picking up garbage on a high traffic street in Dartmouth, my legs nicely scratched from the wild rose bushes, and being pointed at and laughed at by many people walking on the sidewalk, I was coming to an end and was frankly getting a little upset at the reaction received from the people walking in the neighbourhood. In a state of despair over the lack of respect people displayed by littering, I made my last rounds and found one sparkly piece of garbage that caught my attention. When I bent down to pick it up, I realized that it wasn't garbage; it was a $100 bill!

"The fairies truly found a way to reward me that day, and although I haven't found any money since, I never hesitate to venture outside and do my deed."

– Catherine, Dartmouth, Nova Scotia

Fairies are brilliant manifesters. They can assist you in attracting what you desire in your life.

Fairy Tip: Simply ask the fairies for what it is you desire in your life, including material possessions. Then leave it to them to figure out how this will happen. Your job is to simply ask and then follow any intuitive guidance you may receive. What one thing do you desire today? What one dream do you have for yourself? Allow the fairies to help you bring this about in your life. The fairies are there, by your side!

Maritimer Angels:
For Big or Small Needs

Shopping With My Angels

"Finally, I was planning a fun vacation to Florida to briefly escape the Maritimer winter. I needed a break from the snow! I realized I needed a new bathing suit if I was going to Florida as my old bathing suit had seen better days. However, I quickly learned it is not so easy to buy a bathing suit in the middle of winter in Canada. I called upon the angels to help me purchase a new bathing suit.

Days later, while visiting my daughter in Dartmouth, Nova Scotia, I mentioned my bathing suit predicament. My daughter remembered a friend mentioning a store that sold cruise/resort wear year-round. Just the place I was looking for. We headed off to Heatwave Fashions in search of the perfect bathing suit for me. Twenty minutes later, I walked out of the store with two new bathing suits, which I had happily purchased on sale for only $45.

"Thank you, angels, for a quick, easy and cheap purchase for just exactly what I needed!"

– F.D., *Prince Edward Island*

There is nothing too small or too big to ask your angels for, including clothes shopping. Angels do not differentiate between small or big requests. It is all the same to your angels. When you ask for your angels' help, you are not bothering them or taking them away from something more important. So right now, what one small thing would you like to ask your angels' help with? Perhaps you are in a hurry and need all the traffic lights to remain green or you are struggling to find the perfect birthday gift for your grandchild. Maybe you simply need help cooking a new recipe or finding the perfect outfit for a special occasion. Please ask. Your angels are standing by right now waiting to hear your request for help.

Job Hunting with Angels

"I guess you could say the angels helped me out. I asked for a job that I could do out of my home and I ended up with a babysitting job next door. It is only two days a week and the family were willing to work around my schedule. I couldn't have a better job! Thanks, angels."
— *Mary Young, Selma, Nova Scotia*

Angel Message: "We are here to assist you in all ways, even all small ways. Never be afraid to ask for anything as we desire to help you out of love. Please continue to ask us, for you are never a bother to us and we want to lovingly serve your highest needs."

Ask and I Shall Receive

"I was only nineteen years old and going through a difficult time in my life. Financially things were pretty tough. I desperately needed a small amount of extra cash to hold me off until my next payday, two days away. I prayed to God for help. That day, as I was rushing off to work, I found $10 in a puddle (this was over twenty years ago when $10 actually bought me something). I gratefully used this extra money for needed groceries.

"Another day, I asked my angels if they could please provide me with a monthly bus pass to get to and from work. That day at the metro bus station, I looked down and there lying on the ground was a monthly bus pass with no signature on it! I was amazed and extremely grateful for my guardian angel's help."

– L.L., Maritimer Girl

Angel Packing

"I was returning to Prince Edward Island after a fun weekend at White Point Beach, Nova Scotia, with my sisters and mother. My sister, Karen, had lectured the previous day that you can call upon your angels for everything, big or small, to help make your life more peaceful.

"I was sitting in the back seat of the car, with my other sister. Karen asked me to place my overnight bag in the back seat because the trunk was already completely full of luggage. However, I definitely didn't want to endure a long drive squished in with my luggage. As it was, I had driven to White Point Beach uncomfortably wedged in the back seat with my overnight bag between me and my sister. I told Karen, in no uncertain terms, to find room for my overnight bag in the trunk. Karen looked at the overflowing trunk and firmly replied there was simply no room left.

"I was not about to give up. I reminded Karen, 'I heard your talk yesterday. You said we can call upon the angels for anything, including small things. Well, I'm calling upon the angels to find room for this overnight bag in your trunk with everything else!' So Karen also called upon the angels of making luggage fit and she followed the angels' guidance and successfully – and to Karen's surprise – rear-ranged the luggage to fit my overnight bag. Thanks, angels, for the comfortable ride home!

"I had learned the valuable lesson that all I needed to do was simply call upon my angels, even for small things. This just makes my life a whole lot easier, less complicated and peaceful."

– Lesa, Prince Edward Island

Your guardian angels always want to help you in all ways. Take advantage of this! My motto is: If you are not calling upon the angels at least once a day, you are not calling upon them often enough. At any time during the day, consider some small thing you want help with. Then simply ask for it and thank them for their help.

Angel Tip: Always remember to thank the angels/God for their help. These thanks are not because they have an ego that needs to be stroked or to make you feel that you are selfish if you don't thank them. The reason for thanks is that the genuine gratitude behind thanks brings more great blessings into your life. The energetic level behind gratitude is a higher vibration, which attracts even further abundance into your life.

Heavenly Computer Help

"I certainly have never considered myself to be a computer whiz, so I was rather impressed with myself when I arrived at my hotel room and managed to figure out how to set up my laptop and even hook up my laptop to the hotel Internet access. I was on a business conference and, being the overachiever that I am, started working on a business proposal during the evening break. Now I had successfully logged on during lunch to check my e-mails because I always need to be in touch with my customers and never-ending e-mails, so when I went to log on again I was alarmed that I could not turn my computer on.

"I tried not to panic too much. Must just be something stupid, like I my computer was unplugged. I checked the plug – it was plugged in. I even changed the plug to a different outlet beside my hotel desktop, but still no luck. Strangely enough the lamp on the desk was on, so why wasn't my laptop turning on? My laptop was only four months old so I didn't think it was broken. Besides I just used it only hours ago.

"By now I was becoming frustrated and impatient. I couldn't figure out what to do. So finally, I got smart and asked my angels, 'Angels, could you please turn on my laptop for me. I don't know what is wrong with it, but it sure would make my life easier if the stupid thing worked!' I simply sat there for a minute staring at my laptop. I really didn't know how the angels were going to sort this problem out. Then suddenly something was telling me to go turn on the light switch by the hotel room door. This made no sense to me, but I thought, 'Why not?' I turned on the light switch by the door, sat down by my laptop and realized my laptop now had power! I just love how the angels guide me when I ask for their help. Thanks, angels, for getting my laptop up and running again for me!"

– C.C., *Maritimer Forever*

Angel Tip: Any time that you feel frustrated, irritated, angry, anxious and basically are not a happy camper, then that is a hint to you to call upon your angels for help. Remember, your angels are here to bring peace and calmness into your life. If at any point you are not feeling at peace and calm, then that is your cue to call upon your angels no matter how big or small the concern.

Parking Angels

"I have always believed in angels and I love talking to them. One day I was driving downtown in St. John's, Newfoundland, to meet a friend for lunch. I was running late as usual. Now, finding a parking spot downtown on a weekday is not fun, to say the least. I continuously talk to my angels, so without thinking much of it, more talking to myself or so I thought, I told my angels in frustration, 'Angels, look how late I am again. Could you just please make my life easier today by finding me a parking spot right in front of the restaurant?' I honestly was just grumbling to myself when I stated this. But as I drove up to the restaurant, a car pulled out of the only space available to park! I immediately grabbed the parking spot, thanking my angels for not only listening to my rant, but also aiding me in finding a parking spot downtown."

– Laura, St. John's, Newfoundland

Like Laura, I have called upon the angels to help me find a good parking space. I often wonder what will happen when everyone clues into this and everyone starts asking the angels for the perfect place to park. I leave it in the capable hands of the angels. What I have also learned from experience is to give the angels some time to arrange for the parking space to become available. So ask as you leave home or just before arriving at the area you are planning on parking in. Even angels need time to prepare!

Found With Angelic Help

"During an angel workshop, I learned to ask angels for assistance in helping me find any lost object. I was also taught to positively affirm, 'In God's eyes, nothing is lost.' I knew this piece of information would come in handy some day

51

as I have certainly misplaced and lost objects before. Who hasn't lost something?

"One day, while visiting my favourite spa with my friend Shannon, we realized the client before us had misplaced her cell phone. I figured she had been looking for it for at least ten minutes inside the spa, and then she proceeded to go outside and checked to see if she had accidentally dropped it on her way in. While she was desperately looking around outside, I mentioned to Shannon how I had learned not to hesitate in asking angels to help us find lost objects. The woman returned and there was still no sign of her cell phone.

"Both Shannon and I felt sorry for her since we both understood the frustration of losing something. So we decided to help this stranger out. Shannon silently affirmed, 'In God's eyes, nothing is lost.' In the meantime, I silently asked the angels to assist this woman in immediately finding her cell phone. Within thirty seconds the woman began to laugh. She had taken off her coat to once again check her purse. Suddenly she noticed her cell phone in the hood of her coat. I really love the angels' sense of humour when helping us out."

– *Bonnie, Hammonds Plains, Nova Scotia*

Now, who hasn't lost something? Rather than becoming frustrated with needless searching, simply ask the angels to help you find your missing item. The main thing to remember is to trust your intuition as to where you are divinely guided to look. If something is telling you to look in the closet, do not allow your logical mind to say, "But I know I already looked there or I know I didn't place it there." Instead, just simply look in the closet with faith the angels are capable of finding lost items. An item may be lost in our mind, but nothing is lost in God's eyes. The angels will guide you to where the lost item is for angels can manipulate and move lost items to bring the item to you.

Prayer for finding a lost item: Angels, please help me find (name item) quickly and easily. Clearly guide me to where I shall find it. Thank you, angels.

Maritimer Angels:
Nudging You Into Action

A Simple Nudge Home

"I often left my house in the morning rushing off to a meeting. One day as I drove up my road, I looked around the car for my toasted almonds, making sure I had sustenance for later in the day. As I looked around and didn't find them, I saw in my mind the inside of my wood range on fire and filled with big flames. I decided to pay attention and turn around and drive back home.

"I unlocked my house door, rushed over to the stove and carefully opened the oven door. There were large flames from the almonds I'd been toasting the night before, which I had completely forgotten to remove from the oven. Earlier that morning, as I routinely made my coffee and breakfast, I didn't smell anything burning in the stove. The old Enterprise was drafty and quickly heated to a high temperature, so the nuts had lots of time to get burning. Opening the oven door didn't greatly increase the flames because the stove was not airtight and had numerous cracks for air to feed the fire without my help.

"I thanked my angels for nudging me to go back home and ensure more damage was not done! My angels are with me, and so helpful, in some way every day."

– L.H., Maritimer

When you are being nudged into action, pay attention! This nudging is your angels trying to grab your attention. We all have that little voice inside us that we know we should listen to. Listen to this voice. Never ignore your intuition – this is your angels and God communicating with you. Have you ever caught yourself doubting your intuition? We've all been there. We second-guess ourselves; we think too much with our logical minds. Your intuition is a sixth sense, an inner knowing. Here is a prayer to boost your confidence in trusting your intuition.

Prayer to trust your intuition: Angels, please increase my ability to trust my intuition. In trusting my intuition, I trust myself completely. Remove any distrust that my intuition is wrong. Remove any negative patterns I may have learned that prevent me from truly trusting my intuition. Thank you, angels, for my complete confidence in trusting and following my inner guidance.

Soulmate Angels Nudging Me

"I had set myself up on a date with a guy I had met online. I had endured a few of those Internet dates and they all turned out to be less than thrilling. My grandfather was sick in the hospital at the time and I had decided to take a break from bed sitting and call the new guy to have a quick coffee with me. He decided to meet me and I ran home to my parents' home quickly to freshen up. Then I drove to the local coffee shop. I sat in my truck outside and checked my make-up in the mirror. Then I had this overwhelming feeling to leave. I hopelessly asked myself, 'What is the sense of going in here at all? It's probably going to be another idiot and a waste of my time.' I put the visor mirror back up and put my hand on the gear shift to drive away without meeting my date. Then I suddenly felt a squeeze on my shoulder and heard a loving voice firmly say, 'Get out of the truck and go in!' Seeing as how death was all around me at the time with my grandfather on his deathbed and all, I figured that it was my grandmother or my own angels directing me on the right path.

"So with blind faith, I got out of the truck and walked inside to meet my date. As soon as I saw him, my heart dropped to my feet, I lost my breath and just knew from that moment that he was the one that I was supposed to be with through this life. That was five years ago. We became engaged one year after that first date, were married a year after our engagement and had our precious son four months after we married. I believe that voice I heard was my angel guiding me down the path that I had set forth for myself before I came to this life. Since I was so disillusioned with life at the time, I think my angel just needed to nudge me in the right direction."

– *Peggy, Liverpool, Nova Scotia*

Angel Message: "Always listen to your instinct and our gentle nudges, as it is our way of lovingly guiding you on your life's path. We would never lead you astray, as we have your best interests and highest intentions within our hearts."

Angel Nudging for Protection

"In May of 1998, my youngest son and I were about to leave the house to have a fun day at the Discovery Centre. As we were about to walk out the door we both heard water running. Not dripping, but as though the water was being run for a bath. Now, in our house, there were only three places water could come from: the kitchen sink, the bathroom sink and tub, and the sink that was in our basement. We both heard it, so we knew we were not going crazy.

"About fifteen minutes later, the phone rang and my oldest son called from work. He asked what I was up to, and I told him that as soon as we found where the water was coming from, his brother and I would be heading for the Discovery Centre. He asked that we wait for him since he was getting off work and wanted to join us. As soon as I said that we would wait for him at home, the water stopped dripping. Later, my two sons and I were together and we had just exited from the Scotia Square Mall on Duke and Barrington Streets in Halifax. As we walked closer to the TD Bank on Barrington Street, we noticed a group of police officers. Curiously, I inquired what had happened. The police officer told me that if we had have been there thirty minutes sooner, we would have been right in the crossfire of police and bank robbers."

– Shazza, Halifax, Nova Scotia

Your angels are here to protect you from harm's way just as they delayed Shazza and her sons at home so that the family would be safely away from downtown Halifax during a violent crime. But they can only help you if you are following their guidance – guidance that does not always make sense at the time. However, your angels have creative methods of capturing your attention and holding you back from danger. Always listen to your intuition/gut instinct as that is your angels guiding you.

Answered Prayers

Grant's Miracle of Life

"I very clearly remember waking up on June 3, 1998. It struck me that this was going to be an awesome day! I don't ever recall waking up with this kind of feeling before. I wake up each day assuming that it will be a great day and I'll roll along with whatever life deals me. This day, however, would prove to be different. Awesome does not always describe great.

"I went about my usual morning routine. The kids were off to school and I had just finished my first cup of tea when my phone rang. My mother had called to tell me that my brother Grant had been rushed to the hospital. She told me that his wife Rosemary had relayed to her that he had tremendous, uncontrollable pain in his shoulder. I told Mom not to worry. I had just spoken to Grant the night before and his doctor had suggested that he may have a torn rotator in his shoulder. He had been digging a hole in his yard for a hot tub and had just overdone it. She still seemed skeptical but was relieved to hear I had spoken to him of late. I was concerned but not alarmed.

"The phone rang in my Halifax home an hour later. It was Mom again and this time she was in tears. She told me that Grant's liver and kidneys had shut down and it was far more serious than we had imagined. The news riveted through my body and left me numb all over. I just cried, 'Oh, my God' over and over and over again. I told Mom I'd fly home that night to Toronto to be with them.

"As I packed my bags to fly home my heart was shattering into pieces. I grabbed the basics and tossed them into my suitcase. What about the funeral? What would I wear to that? Stop it! My mind was racing much faster than I could cope with the thoughts. I dropped to my knees and prayed with everything I had that God would save my brother ... but from what? What shoulder injury would leave his body in full renal failure? What were the doctors not telling us? I called the Sunnybrook Health Sciences Centre and asked to speak with his attending physician. I could not believe the compassion that Dr. Forrest showed me on the phone. He took the time to speak with me; however, he was also uncertain of Grant's condition. He was paged to Grant's side and I would not speak to him again until I arrived in Toronto.

"My best friend Allison met me at the airport and without hesitation we were off to the hospital. I walked in to find my family paralyzed with fear. We were quickly taken to the consult room, which I soon named the 'dark room.' You never get good news from the 'dark room.'

"The head nurse looked very grim as she told us of Grant's serious condition. She called it necrotizing fasciitis. Necrotizing what? She reduced it to a term we all understood. Flesh-eating disease! I attempted to remain calm and unfazed by this news. I was crumbling inside as I was processing the thought. She said that my brother had a ten percent chance of surviving this. His condition was very unstable and he was in the trauma unit recovering from a massive debridement Dr. Forrest had done earlier on in the day. I steeled myself while Rosemary took me in to see Grant.

"The trauma unit was a series of several beds in a darkened area. At the end of this unit was a bed under full lights and confusion. It was surrounded by a relay team of several nurses and doctors who appeared to be working frantically. I couldn't imagine who might need all of this attention so late at night. As I neared the bed I soon realized that it was Grant's bed. It was like watching a finely tuned orchestra in motion. Once again I buried my fear from sight and approached him without hesitation. Norma was in control of his care and she readily invited me to be with him as long as I needed to.

"Grant was swollen to three times his regular size. His eyes were bulging out and there was little definition between his neck and his head. I was told he was on a drug to paralyze him so that he would not waste any precious energy needed to beat this disease. I held his hand and continued to talk to him throughout the night. He felt like plastic and we watched as his fingers and toes turned black from the lack of circulation. Pumps beeped, dialysis machines hummed and nurses changed bag after bag of IV fluids.

"All the while I continued to tell him that I knew something good would come from all of this. I didn't know what, but something good would definitely come from all of this. We just had to be patient. I told the nurses that they clearly did not know who they were dealing with. I told them that Grant was a fighter and that if anyone could beat this, he would. All the while I wondered how this horrible bacterium could have entered into such a tiny scratch on his arm and left him so battered and bruised.

"After a week I regretfully flew home to Halifax. I cried as the plane taxied down the runway. How could I leave my brother in still such critical circumstances? I was convinced that he knew I was there even though he lay there in a deep coma day after day.

"Two weeks later my sister-in-law, Rosemary, called me in the wee hours of the morning. She was on her cell phone and was frantically racing to the hospital. The doctor had called her and told her to get to the hospital as soon as possible. Grant's vitals were crashing. He was not going to make it. I talked her all the way into the elevator. She called me later to say that he had stabilized. Thank God. Then two hours later she called again. This time she said that the doctor had called once again. She said that Grant had suffered with only thirty percent oxygen to his brain for over twenty minutes. They were sure he was brain-damaged. She was told not to attempt to make it to the hospital as he would be gone in five to thirty minutes. They said he would have a massive heart attack and it would be all over. Please make the funeral arrangements.

"Rosemary and I agreed that considering his brain was damaged and his kidneys would be on indefinite dialysis, this would be the better alternative for Grant. It was certain that even if he survived he would lose his fingers and toes to amputation and that he would have to be on a transplant list for his kidneys. He would never cope being physically or mentally severely compromised. We agreed not to resuscitate him. After all, we were acting in his best interest. Or were we? Was it his pain we wanted to end or was it ours? He was incapable of feeling anything at this point. But nothing could measure the immense pain we were experiencing.

"I told Rosemary that I would call Mom and Dad. I would be the one to tell them that their son was soon to die. I would also call our older brother Ross and let him know the inevitable outcome of the day. These were the hardest calls I would ever have to make but they were not ones I felt Rosemary should have to make.

"Meanwhile, my brother Ross and his family were in church praying for Grant's recovery. A couple approached Ross and introduced themselves as the parents of a young boy who had died just ten days before of necrotizing fasciitis. Diana and Martin had never met Ross, nor had they ever been to their church before. Diana promised to go home and pray for Grant's life.

"After a half an hour passed I began to grieve Grant's death. I sat motionless out on my deck and I looked deep into the passing clouds. Where was he right now? Was he watching over me? I pondered over heaven and wondered if they were really ready for him or not! I waited for my husband David to come home from an overnight camping trip with our son Leslie. I told him the news as soon as he came in. My husband denied it and said it couldn't be. I kept hearing myself say to him, 'It's over!' Those words echoed from my lips each time I said them. I was on the outside looking in. It was almost like an out-of-body experience. I went all day believing that he was dead only to receive a phone call later that day to say Grant was still alive!

"My emotions had been stretched further than a rubber band. How could the doctors play with our emotions like this? I stood in the shower as the steam filled the air and I yelled to my God in heaven. 'What are you doing?! Make up your mind! If you're going to take him then take him! But if you're going to let him stay then make him better, but whatever you do ... make up your mind!' I was so angry with God. What kind of a God would allow Grant to suffer like this and at the same time play such wicked games with our emotions?

"The following day Grant remained in extremely critical condition. I could barely function. I called a friend of mine who gave me the number to a prayer group in the United States. She told me that anyone who had ever called it received such great results. I quickly hung up and called the number. A very kind gentleman prayed for God's will in Grant's care. I held Grant's picture close to my heart as I finally fell to sleep.

"When I woke up I literally jumped out of bed. I knew that some divine intervention had happened in Grant's life. Somehow I just knew he would be okay. It was an unbelievable calm that had come to erase my raw emotions. Even though all the odds were against my brother Grant, I was certain his life was in good hands. It was not until several months later I would realize that an angel had come to tell me of Grant's fate.

"Grant surpassed unbelievable odds as the months ticked by. He was on full life support for over two months. He would recover from one infection only to be quickly invaded by another. The doctors were running out of available antibiotics. His body had declared germ warfare. His white blood cells were raging out of control. He eventually started to gain some strength and positive signs of improvement, which were followed by heart failure. This was the one organ we were not worried about. As the nurses struggled to keep his heart working, he went into a brain seizure which carried on for four minutes. Once again the family was left with little hope. I, on the other hand, knew something they didn't. After all, an angel told me so!

"The head neurologist said that Grant's MRI was the worst he had ever read in the hospital. His brain was totally damaged and was not expected to recover. Yet that was not to be. Within twenty-four hours Grant was sitting up asking very intelligent questions! Once again the medical staff scratched their heads. What is it with this guy?!

"In early September, Grant was released from the hospital and sent home walking with a cane. He has been declared a miracle at the Sunnybrook Health Sciences Centre! The doctors have agreed that it was indeed divine intervention that saved Grant Drummond.

"While my family was enduring this awful drama I

retired night after night to the Internet. There I would find comfort from people who had survived this awful disease. I vowed that if my brother were allowed to live, I would volunteer my time on the National Necrotizing Fasciitis Foundation site. I lived up to my vow and continued to scan the site each day for people who might be going through the early stages of this frightening disease. Not one person would go through this alone if I could do something about it.

It was there that I saw a posting from Diana Cahill. I was sure she was the same person my brother Ross had met in church weeks before. I took a chance and wrote to her. I introduced myself as just a caring person who had been aware of her son Matthew's death. I told her how sorry I was for her loss but that I wanted her to know that a divine presence had visited me and told me that my brother would be okay. I was trying to assure her that her son Matt is likely up in heaven looking down on her right now.

"Diana wrote to me the next day and confirmed that she in fact was the person my brother had met. She told me that she had gone home and prayed to her deceased son Matt to go and find Grant in his spiritual travels. She prayed that Matt would encourage Grant to turn back and to fight for his life. She was determined to see Matt save at least one life from the hideous disease that had taken his young life of seventeen years. As I read her letter my heart opened up and I cried uncontrollably. I knew at that moment that it had been Diana's son Matthew who had visited me. How emotional it was for me to accept that a young boy had died and that he would be so instrumental in letting my brother of forty-three years live! Was that really how God's plan worked? But wait. I needed to know exactly when Diana had said her prayers. When did she contact Matthew and pray for his involvement with Grant?

"It took several hours before I could compose myself enough to write to Diana again. I cautiously asked her if she remembered when she had met Ross at church and what date was it that she prayed to Matt to help us. I was certain I knew the answers to these questions but I had to ask none the less. Diana confirmed the date as being June 23, 1998. This was exactly the time of my divine encounter. Overwhelmed does not begin to describe the feelings I had of our discovery. Not only did I know the name and identity of my messenger, but I had also come face to face with his mother. Make no mistake about it. This is all by design. This is all part of the plan. All part of God's seemingly awkward but none the less perfect plan.

"My encounter with Diana has established a relationship with a stranger that will stand the test of time. We are connected by a bond so tight that nothing could break it. While it is only held together by faith we both know it wasn't a coincidence that we met. We understand that coincidences purely do not exist. There is a reason for everything. It is all part of the plan. When I told Grant that something very good would come from this, little did I know that the good would come to me."

– Ann Perry, Nova Scotia

I love Ann's story as it beautifully illustrates the power of prayer and the power of hope. When you pray, I encourage you to pray straight from your heart. Prayer is personal. It is not necessary for prayer to be flowery in words, invoked in a specific way or even a long-drawn-out affair. Simply pray from your heart. Pray to who you feel comfortable with in the spiritual world. This is a personal choice dependent on your spiritual and/or religious beliefs. You decide who you wish to pray to. I believe in the power of prayers and encourage you to never underestimate the power of your prayers and the amazing difference they make.

Leave your worry behind, for worry is only negative energy you are sending to someone else and affirming what you don't want. If you truly yearn to help someone else, ditch the worry and pray for them instead. You can influence a healing difference in this world and in someone else's life through your heartfelt prayers. When you pray straight from your heart, you are connecting directly with divine intervention to intercede on your behalf.

Home Safe Home

"In February 2006, I was involved in a single car accident that resulted in my car being completely written off. Thankfully, I was not injured, but I certainly lost my nerve for driving in winter storms.

"The following February 2007, I found myself having to once again drive home during a snowstorm. I was absolutely terrified. Throughout the late afternoon and into the evening the snow continued falling. I started praying to God and my angels to please get me home safely. I was unable to change my clients' appointments and felt I needed to stay at my hair salon. As it turned out all my clients showed up that afternoon and I didn't want to reschedule or disappoint any of them.

"Driving home, after a busy work day, I continued to pray and asked my angels to guide me and keep me safe during my drive home on the snowy roads. After driving for twenty minutes, I came close to the area where I had my car accident last year. I was practically in tears as I desperately wanted to avoid yet another car accident. I felt the grips of fear wave through me yet again. I was about to pull over when suddenly I felt a strong sense of calmness and peacefulness flow over my entire body. Along with this calmness I felt a great strength of courage deep within me.

I remember reassuring myself, 'I'm going to make it home safely.'

"I wondered where this new-found courage came from. Just then, from the corner of my eye, I noticed what I thought was a white bird, maybe a pigeon. I just wasn't sure exactly what I noticed as it was so unexpected. Yet it was floating in front of my car and then just as quickly disappeared from view towards the sea. So I thought to myself, 'If a pigeon (or whatever bird that was I saw) could make it in this stormy weather, then so could I!'

"So I carried on driving, determined to make it home safely and feeling at peace that I would. Just as I drove around a turn in the road, I couldn't believe my eyes! The twisty, turning piece of highway where my car accident occurred last year was completely clear of snow, even though it was still storming outside. The road was wet as if it had been raining, but not a single speck of snow was on the highway for the next two kilometres. When I came out of the section of turns, the heavy snow began; however, the road was straight and well lighted with street lights.

"It then became very clear to me that the white object that I originally thought was a pigeon or other bird was actually an angel. This angel ensured my safe drive home and infused me with the courage to continue driving home that night. I am forever grateful for my angel's assistance in clearing and lighting my path home!"

– Siggie Frosst, Nova Scotia

It is the greatest desire of our angels to help us in our lives. However, we must learn to ask for angelic and divine help. This is not because the angels are being picky or demanding, but because the Law of Free Will prevails. The Law of Free Will stipulates we are able to make our own choices in our lives, including asking for divine help. Angels and God do not dictate what we must do. They offer loving guidance when we ask for this and it is our choice if we accept the guidance or not. Either way, we are not judged for our decisions.

Angel Message: "Know that we would never interfere with your lives as you desire to live them. If you need our help in any way, please ask us for it is our greatest joy to assist you. There is no special way of asking. Just even think of us and we are instantly by your side, ready to serve."

Angel Tip: To assist you in remembering to ask the angels for help, write on a piece of paper, "Angels, I could really use your help with ..." Then place this in a prominent place such as your wallet, car dashboard, fridge, or bathroom mirror, for frequent reminding. When I was first trying to remember to ask the angels for help more often, I wrote this note to myself and carried it around in my wallet for a few months. Now, I am habitually calling upon my angels for guidance.

Perfect Home

"I was seeking angelic guidance in buying the perfect home for me and my family. During an angel session in 2007, Karen called upon the angels of house finding and said a prayer for our family to be provided with a spacious house with two bathrooms close to our farm – just the type of home we were seeking.

"The following evening at 6:30, I received a phone call from a person I had been in touch with a year before. She wanted to meet with me as soon as possible. I met with her at 7:30 a.m. on the following Sunday morning. She had been through a recent separation. I had originally called her in October 2006 because I heard that she might be interested in selling her farm. (It is a house and organic farm). At the time she wasn't interested or ready to sell.

"In January 2007 she called me back as she was ready to sell; however, she was asking more money than we could consider paying. I told her that I hoped she would be able to sell it for her asking price but that it wasn't something I could currently afford. Over the months, I noticed she listed the property.

"When she called on the Saturday evening I agreed to meet with her. At our early morning meeting she was telling me that she really wanted to sell the farm to someone who she knew would farm it and properly care for the land as she originally envisioned. I assured her I was still very interested and would definitely respect the land, but explained I could not pay the price she was asking. I then told her my price range.

"During the next week she obviously seriously considered my offer because she decided to accept it, knowing I would properly care for and respect the farmland. I am pleased that my desired house came about and that we have this precious farmland. I am grateful for the angels' amazing role in providing me my home and farmland."

– *Patricia Bishop, Nova Scotia*

Buying or selling a house? Don't forget to call upon the angels in assisting you in selling and buying your home.

House-selling prayer: Angels, help me to sell my home quickly, easily and for the full asking price or better. Clearly guide me as to what work on the house I may need to do to help it sell. Please bring the right family to this home. Thank you, angels.

House-buying prayer: Angels, please help me purchase the best house, most suitable for me and my family. We desire our new home to be (specifically list what you are looking for in size, bedrooms, bathrooms, garage and so on.) Help us determine which area to buy in. Help us find the best real estate agent. Thank you, angels, for our beautiful new home.

Angelic Pain Relief

"I was sincerely concerned about my birth mother's health for she had recently undergone serious surgery. Since the surgery she had been bedridden due to acute pain in both her legs. My mother has arthritis and due to the surgery she had to temporarily discontinue her arthritic pain medications. I felt terrible that she was enduring such pain and discomfort.

"I sat with her to keep her company and to distract her from her pain. Yet I felt compelled to help comfort her in other ways. I believe in angels and have sought their help in the past. This time I needed the angels to assist my mother. I silently asked Archangel Raphael to completely ease my mother's pain. I knew he is the healing angel and healing was definitely needed. Then I offered my mother Reiki, a form of energy healing.

"My mother softly and comfortably fell asleep for the next thirty minutes. When she woke up, she immediately commented on how much better she felt. In fact, she decided to sit up and then proceeded to stand up by herself. Until then, it took two nurses to assist my mother out of bed. The nurses, I and my mother were very surprised that she recuperated to moving on her own so quickly. The next day she was up walking the halls by herself, no longer suffering from debilitating arthritic pain.

"I am constantly amazed by how powerful angels' help can be. I wanted to share this story so that you too can know to call upon your angels to help you in your life."

– *Bonnie, Nova Scotia*

As demonstrated by Bonnie, you can ask the angels to help other people. The angels then go to the higher being of the other person, that part of you free from fear and connected to the divine, and ask if he/she would like to receive angelic help. The angels never do anything against your will. If you agree to their help, they will help you. If you decline their help, which in my experience is rare, then the angels will respect your decision.

Archangel Raphael's Message: "For any healing concerns, whether they are physical, mental, emotional or spiritual, never hesitate to call upon me to assist you. You deserve Divine healing energy in all aspects of your life. You need simply think of angels and we are immediately by your side."

Angel Tip: Archangel Raphael's aura colour is green, representing healing. If you want to help someone in physical pain, along with calling upon Archangel Raphael, envision the person surrounded by a beautiful, emerald green light. As a guideline, take five to ten minutes twice a day to visualize this. This light invokes divine healing. You can also do this visualization for yourself.

Deceased Loved Ones: By Our Side

Butterfly Sign

"A few days after my brother, Leo, died I was sitting on my backyard under my covered, canopied deck in the beginning of June. Suddenly, a beautiful tiger swallowtail butterfly swooped very close around me and flew around my head. I suddenly wondered, 'Is that my brother, Leo, sending me a message?' I felt there was something to it as butterflies don't normally fly so close in this swooping manner. In my heart I believed it was my deceased brother, whom I was close to, assuring me he is okay and to stop worrying about him.

"At the time I was first visited by this butterfly, I was babysitting a young girl who also noticed this beautiful, large butterfly, which is not normally seen around my area. The second year of the anniversary of Leo's death, I was sitting outside babysitting when once again the same tiger swallowtail butterfly I had seen last year gently swooped around my head and yard. The young girl I was babysitting exclaimed, 'Look, there is your brother!' I felt Leo's peaceful presence.

"The third year of the anniversary of Leo's death, I was relaxing outside with my adult daughter, Charlene, when we both noticed the return of the tiger swallowtail gently swooping around us as if to say hello. It was Charlene who recognized and explained to me that a tiger swallowtail butterfly legendarily holds a person's soul.

"Each year, I now expect to see this tiger swallowtail as my brother's way of saying 'hello' and letting me know he is at peace."

– Loretta, Nova Scotia

Our deceased loved ones often find creative ways to send us a message reassuring us that they are well and at peace. One common sign from a deceased loved one is through butterflies and birds (and other animals). The butterfly or bird will stand out because it will fly closer to you than normal and act out of character, for example sitting still longer or looking at you directly. Also, as you admire the butterfly or bird, you will suddenly be reminded of your deceased loved one and feel a sensation of peace overflow your body. Always trust that it is a sign from your deceased loved one. You are not making it up! As most people are clairsentient (they can feel things), we can easily feel the loving presence of our deceased loved ones.

Remembering Dad's Love

"I was having a day where I felt I was on cloud nine! I had just registered my new healing business, been accepted into massage school and my life was falling into place in following my life purpose. It was an exciting time for me.

"Now get this, as I was driving home after successfully registering my healing business, I was thinking about my deceased dad in his final hours here on earth. I remember wanting to make him as comfortable as possible. At the time, without speaking, I felt Dad was telling me things that would make him feel more comfortable in his final hours, or maybe it was just that I was thinking about what I'd want if I were in his shoes. In between the Reiki treatments, a form of energy healing, I was massaging my dad's hands and limbs as they started to turn blue. The need to heal has always been innate with me, just waiting to be expressed, and I believed this long before I became a Reiki practitioner.

"Anyway, as I was experiencing this little flashback in the car, seconds later a song came on the car radio and I started to cry. Yeah, right in the middle of traffic – total basket case. Large tears rolled down my face. It was the same song I played at Dad's memorial presentation. The song by Sarah McLachlan was titled 'I Will Remember You.' I really felt like Dad was with me right then and there, so much so I told him I loved him. Then I felt Dad's tender hand on my shoulder. How emotional this was for me! But in a good way! Now if anyone told me how much healing and forgiving I was going to go through this year, I would have thought they were nuts. But now it all makes sense and leaves my heart a little bit lighter."

– Brad Surette, Halifax, Nova Scotia

Another sign from our deceased loved ones is through radio songs. If a song comes on the radio at a time when you need to know your loved one is around and this song has special significance with your loved one – trust it is your loved one saying hello and sending their love. If a song has certain words jumping out at you, and you suddenly think of your deceased loved ones, it is them. It is not a mere coincidence. They are by your side. Deceased people work with vibrations; therefore, they are able to easily manipulate electricity since electricity is a form of vibration. They frequently use the radio to capture your attention.

Matchmaking From Heaven

"Three years ago my husband, who was in very good health, left home one Saturday morning to play baseball. Suddenly, he suffered a massive heart attack on the ball field and never returned home. Our love for each other after thirty-eight years of marriage was still very deep and I thought my life was over. I went into shock and deep mourning for a year. I loved what we shared and yearned for the deep love that I felt from my husband and our special life together. One lonely night I wrote a letter to my husband telling him how I felt and I asked him to find me someone who would fulfill all that I missed in marriage. I specifically wrote down the qualities I was looking for in a new partner and new life.

"My husband had formed a ball league twenty-five years previously and a league reunion had been planned. It was also a night that would be a tribute to my deceased husband. My friend called me about three days prior to the reunion and asked if I was going. I told my friend I was unaware of this reunion. She informed me that no one knew how to contact me as I had sold my home after my husband's death and moved in with my adult daughter. The mailed invitation had been returned. She almost didn't call me as she had assumed I knew about the reunion through another friend.

"I decided to attend to honour my husband's memory. I went to the dance and reunited with a lot of our old friends. One in particular asked me if I was attending the ball game the next morning. I replied I didn't know there was one, but probably would attend. He told me it would start at 10 a.m. I arrived at 10 a.m. and there wasn't a game, but this was the field where my husband had died and I was pleased to be alone as I had never returned after a friend reenacted my husband's last moments with me.

75

This was precious time to heal, reminisce and feel my husband's presence.

"It turned out the time had changed to 11 a.m. and my friend was not aware of it. After awhile people started to arrive and my male friend arrived, apologizing for the mix-up in timing. I simply replied, 'It was meant to be as it gave me time to be with my deceased husband.' He was not aware that this was the field my husband had died at. We sat on the bench and effortlessly talked throughout the game about my husband's death and his painful recent marital separation after thirty-two years of marriage. He told me that he had originally made up his mind not to attend the ball league reunion (he lives in Moncton) and was originally scheduled to attend a ninetieth birthday party. However, just hours before the party, he found himself in his car driving towards Halifax. He was puzzled as to why he suddenly changed his mind, but felt it must have been the right choice since he would have to see these people eventually and endure the explanation that he was longer with his wife.

"To shorten this story, I will fast forward and tell you that we are now, two years later, planning to be married. We are both convinced that there was divine intervention on that day, as he did things in the days and months that followed that were not at all like him, but were instrumental in the development of our relationship.

"My husband's life ended on that field and my new life began on that field, just two weeks before the first anniversary of his death. Did this man have all the qualities I had written to my husband? Absolutely! Are we happy? Absolutely! It has been a very healing journey for us both as he also lost someone that he (thought) he loved after thirty-two years. But he says I am his angel and a miracle. He only dreamt of this kind of happiness. No one will ever convince him or me that someone didn't push him all the way to Halifax, from New Brunswick, to me. There are no coincidences.

"I completely believe that our deceased loved ones do take care of us from the other side. I've experienced it and give gratitude. I am very blessed."

– Lise Coleman, Moncton, New Brunswick

Please know that along with your angels and God, our deceased loved ones are by our sides, ready to help and guide us. Even in the afterlife, they can lovingly assist us. Just simply talk to them as though they are here. Let them know what you need them to help you with. There are no special words to be said. Truly speak from your heart. It's all in the asking and giving them permission to help you. Remember, you have a whole team of deceased loved ones, ready to assist you at any time. They may be deceased, but they are still with us in spirit.

Peter's Roses

"During a workshop on learning to receive messages from your angels, I doubted if I was actually receiving any messages. While practising receiving a message, I saw a beautiful red glow while simultaneously smelling roses. I later realized that my angels were connecting me to my deceased younger brother, Peter. Peter had died suddenly in the hospital and I desperately missed his presence. His death was a heartache for me.

"At a later date, I was walking up my driveway and silently asked Peter if I was doing the right thing by talking to a lawyer concerning a lawsuit surrounding his death. As I continued walking up my driveway, I glanced over at a rose bush which my daughter had thoughtfully bought me in remembrance of Peter. This rose bush was in full bloom! Yet I had checked this rose bush earlier in the morning and at that time the buds were not even trying to bloom. I had been closely watching the rose bush as I was excited to see the yellow and pink blooms. I knew right away it was Peter's sign for me that I was going in the right direction.

"I attended a funeral wake for a close friend's mother. This was the first wake I attended since my younger brother's death. When I stepped out of my car, I suddenly smelled a strong scent of roses. My husband, who was standing directly beside me, could not smell these roses. Again, I really believed Peter was telling me he is okay.

"This all connects to the day after Peter's funeral when I dreamt about a dozen red roses. As I drove back to Halifax, from Peter's funeral in Prince Edward Island, I felt a very strong feeling to buy Peter's girlfriend a dozen roses, which I did. She called the next day and explained to me that Peter had given her a dozen roses for Christmas (weeks before he died) unknown to me. She cried, but was very happy to receive these roses as they were a loving reminder of Peter.

"This is my rose story and I thank the angels for connecting me to my brother Peter."
– *Patricia Phelan, Sackville, Nova Scotia*

Coping with the death of a loved one can be difficult as you miss them tremendously. If you are grieving the death of a loved one, ask them for a sign that they are around you. They will gladly provide you with a sign, reassuring you of their caring presence. There are many ways your loved ones can provide signs. You might, for example, notice lights flickering on and off. You may feel their presence beside you, touching your shoulder, dream of them or smell something that reminds you of them, such as perfume, baked cookies or flowers. Trust the sign that you receive. You are not making it up.

Our deceased loved ones are never alone. They are surrounded by angels, God and other deceased relatives.

Angel Message: "Know that your deceased loved ones are with us here in heaven. They are doing well. They are completely surrounded by peace and love. Please do not mourn their death, for they have not died in spirit. Your loved ones send all their love to you. They are safe in our care. They are close to your heart."

Pink Roses From Chantal

"The year of 2003 was long and hard for my family. In January of 2003 I was placed off work early by my doctor because of problems I was having during my third pregnancy. It was usually I who made sure beds were made, carpets were vacuumed and bills were paid on time, but this winter I could not handle any of these everyday chores. I felt like I had spent almost three months lying on my side sick in bed, exhausted from my pregnancy. My inner instincts knew there was trouble ahead and I felt I had to do all I could to save my precious baby.

"I remember asking my father once if he had a favourite child and he replied, 'Yes I do.' This was quite a shock to us children, because we were not aware of who the favourite child was. I have one younger brother and two older sisters. We are a loving, close-knit family and grew up knowing our parents loved us all equally. So when we asked him who was this supposed favourite child, Dad smilingly replied, 'Whoever needs me the most.' I now knew what he meant, because my two young boys were not receiving all the attention they normally would from me, as I needed so much rest to look after my unborn child, the one 'who needed me most.'

"March of 2003 came and unfortunately Chantal never lived past her first day on earth, and with a pain I cannot describe to anybody, and only those who go through it can understand, we buried our dear little girl. My instinct had been right; she had needed more help than I could ever give her.

"It was our strong faith in God which kept my husband and me going. So many people made comments of how well we were doing, keeping it together after Chantal's death. If they only knew how untrue that was. Shortly after I came home from the hospital I was up in the middle of the night again crying and trying to deal with this heart-wrenching grief. I prayed to God to give me a sign that my baby girl was all right. When I was walking back to bed I noticed the pink rose begonia plant my husband had given to me after Chantal died had come in full bloom. I made a promise to my daughter right then and there that whenever I observed a pink rose I would know it was her way of reaching out to me and saying 'Hello.'

"The next morning my older sister, Rhonda, told me Mom had heard from our cousins. Betty lived in Montreal so we did not have frequent contact with her. Betty had a dream where my grandmother Bessie MacKinnon along with her husband Neil were reaching out to receive a baby girl all dressed in pink. Betty knew I was pregnant and phoned home to her sisters to see how I was doing and tell them of her surprising dream. It was then she learned our baby girl had died during labour and delivery. My mother talked to her about the dream and asked her what colour hair the baby had. Betty did not know as the baby was adorned in a pink bonnet and she was lovingly wrapped in a beautiful pink blanket. This was the way we buried our dear little girl. I knew this was a sign from God that my little girl was in heaven and my deceased grandparents were looking after her. It was a relief to know Chantal was met and being taken care of by my deceased grandparents.

"As for the pink roses, they have come to me in so many different ways and at various times and I have always known the pink roses are Chantal saying 'hello' or 'everything is going to be all right.' One particular time my husband, Wayne, had been rushed to the hospital and obviously I was very upset worrying about him. As I was walking in the hospital doors, three people in a row walked out, each carrying a pink rose.

"Writing the above story was obviously very emotional and hard for me to do. After typing the story I tried to e-mail it to Karen; however, for some reason I could not attach the story and send the e-mail. I reread the story and thought it was awhile since I had seen a pink rose from Chantal.

"The next day I opened an e-mail from my friend Shirley. The e-mail was a story of a little girl who had saved her mother's life even though the little girl was in heaven. The 'wallpaper' to the story had beautiful pink roses and the background music was 'Angels Among Us' by Alabama, a song dear to my family, and the one we had played at my father's funeral. I knew this was Chantal once again telling me everything was going to be all right."

– Lesa Murnaghan, Prince Edward Island

It can be emotionally difficult for those left behind here on earth when a loved one dies, especially a child. You can certainly ask God and the angels to give you a sign that your deceased loved one is doing well in the afterlife. Your angels understand your need to know for sure your deceased loved one is doing well. Just simply ask God/your angels: "God, my angels, please give me a sign that (name person) is doing well in their afterlife. Let me know for certain that they are well." Then trust the sign you receive. I cannot say often enough that you are not making the sign up.

When our loved ones, including children, die, they are absolutely not alone in this process. They are lovingly greeted by their guardian angels, God and other loved ones who died before them. All greet our deceased loved ones with open arms and complete, unconditional love.

Angel Tip: Archangel Azrael's role is to assist people in crossing over to the afterlife – that is, going to the other side or heaven. His name means "whom God helps" and he is known in the Hebrew and Muslim religions; however, you can be of any religious/spiritual belief to work with him. If someone has recently died you can call upon Archangel Azrael to be with your deceased loved one during their spiritual transition. You can also call upon Archangel Azrael to help you heal through your own grieving process. Example: Archangel Azrael, my heart is grieving over the death of (name person). Please help me through this grieving process and help me heal my heart. Let me remember all the good of this person and the fun times we have had. Help me not stay focused on only their death. Let me feel peace and your comforting presence. Thank you.

Kids and Angels

Sleeping Safe

"I asked Archangel Michael to not have nightmares so I can be safe sleeping. I said it in my head. I felt safe and have no nightmares now. I can't see angels. I can feel angels around me."

– six-year-old boy, Prince Edward Island

To help prevent your children and you from experiencing nightmares at night, call upon Archangel Michael to protect your children during their sleep. You can also teach your children to call upon the angels to protect them during their sleep.

Prayer for Peaceful Sleep: Archangel Michael and my guardian angels, please guard over and protect me during my sleep. Keep me safe from all harm. Let me dream only peaceful dreams during my sleep tonight. Thank you, angels.

In God's Light

"I asked God to surround me in light and I now feel safe."
– Brodie Murnaghan, age six
Donagh, Prince Edward Island

Angel Tip: Have you ever felt unsafe or unprotected? Then do just exactly what Brodie did and ask God/angels to surround you in white light. Now quietly sit with this divine white light completely surrounding you. Notice how you immediately feel safe, protected and peaceful. That's how powerful divine energy is. I recommend invoking this light around you at the beginning of each day to feel the loving divine energy surrounding and protecting you. What a great way to start your day – even better than a cup of coffee.

Behaving Myself with the Angels' Help

"Sometimes I ask angels to help me to be good during the day and I am."

– Brodie, age six

Guardian Angel Message for Children: "May you always feel our love for you shine bright like a star in the sky. We love it when you talk to us, for we are always right beside you. If we can help you in any way, let us know. You can talk to us aloud or think what you want us to know and we will hear you instantly. We love you very deeply and you are very precious in our eyes."

My Halloween Story

"It was Halloween Day and I couldn't find my Halloween mask. I asked the angels if they could find it, but it was time to go to school. So I asked the angels to help my mom to look for it for me. I asked the angels again just before I left school. Once I got back home from school my mom had found my mask. It made me happy and I had fun on Halloween trick or treating. I got two bags of candy."

> *– Austin Murnaghan, age eight*
> *Donagh, Prince Edward Island*

I love hearing stories of children calling upon the angels to assist them in their lives. One of the most precious spiritual gifts you can give children is to encourage them to call upon their angels. If they are old enough to talk, they are old enough to connect with their angels and God. Children are far more open to angelic messages as they have not learned to mistrust their intuition or block out their inherent spiritual gifts. One children's angel book I highly recommend is *Thank You Angels* by Doreen Virtue.

Special Person

"I always like being picked as the 'special person' in my class. The 'special person' gets to help the teacher for that week and be in front of the line. I asked the angels for my name to be picked as 'special person.' It made me excited when my name was picked."

> *– Austin, age eight*

Angel Tip for Children: It is easy to ask your angels for help. Just simply ask them for what you need, just like you would ask your parents. You can think of what you want, say it aloud, write it down or pray for it. Whichever way works for you! Then let the angels do their work in helping you. They will gladly assist you. Don't forget to thank them for their help.

Going to the Movies

I have learned how helpful the angels can be when babysitting my two young nephews. Here is an example of how the angels assisted me in looking good in my nephews' eyes.

I was taking my young nephews to see the latest popular children's movie, *Shrek the Third*. It was the first weekend the movie was playing and I was worrying we might not even get a ticket as silly me didn't pre-purchase the ticket. It was a rainy Saturday afternoon and every other parent (and aunt like me) had the same idea of taking their children out to the movies. Unfortunately, my nephews remembered the last time I attempted to take them to a popular children's movie and the tickets were sold out.

As we pulled into the parkway of the movie theatre, I heard one of my nephews praying, 'Please angels, let us get into this movie today. I really want to see this movie and Aunt Karen isn't here tomorrow to take us. [I was visiting from out of province and leaving the next day.] Thank you, angels, for getting us into the movie!' We walked into the extremely overcrowded theatre and stood in a long line to purchase our tickets. By then, I was also asking the angels help in getting us tickets because I did not want to disappoint my nephews yet again. Finally, we reached the ticket agent. I asked for three tickets and the ticket agent told me I was lucky as there were literally only a few seats left for *Shrek the Third* that day – even the evening shows were beginning to sell out.

Thanks, angels, for looking out for us!

"Thank you, angels, for getting us into the movie!" is a perfect example of a heartfelt affirmation. One aspect of asking for angelic assistance is to affirm what you desire. Positively affirm what you desire as though it has already happened. For example, if you have an arthritic knee affirm, "Thank you, angels, for my healed knee moving in all directions in comfort." If you have a sore or bad back, affirm, "Thank you, angels, for my strong back that supports my complete body movement." If you are seeking a pay raise, affirm, "Thank you, angels, for my fifteen percent pay raise." Be careful not to affirm in the negative. For example refrain from saying, "I no longer want knee pain. I no longer want to suffer."

Your thoughts are extremely powerful. Part of the Law of Attraction is that what you think about, you bring about. Therefore, positive affirmations plant in your own mind what it is you truly desire, rather than focusing on what you don't desire. Use your thoughts to your advantage.

Angel Poems: Just For You

Believe

If we just light the fire in our soul,
We can heal the planet as a whole,
Find the light and love within your heart,
And believe we can make a brand new start.

We all have the power within us,
If we just focus and believe,
That there truly is no limit,
If we just plant the seed.

Close your eyes and find the place,
Where you feel gratitude and love,
And let the light shine from within your soul,
To the Universe above.

It only takes one tiny step,
To make a difference in our lives,
Just imagine what all of us can do,
To make a difference worldwide.

Find the song within your heart,
And sing it everyday,
And remember that healing is only one thought away.

When you find yourself feeling down,
And don't know what to do,
Look inside yourself to find the truth,
And remember that you have the power within you.

The angels are all around us,
They help us on our way,
Guiding us with the words,
When we don't know what to say.

Just when you think it's over,
And there is no end in sight,
They fill us with their energy and beautiful white light.

They all come in different forms,
But they have a familiar way
Of providing us with exactly what we need
To help us on our way.

If we could all be open,
And be truly ready to see,
We would recognize the miracles
That are surrounding you and me.

If you ever sit and listen,
And hear the whispers in your ear,
You'll realize it's the angels,
Telling you that they're here.

Trust that voice you're hearing,
And believe with all of your heart
That the truth is within you,
And it's been there from the start.

Be proud of how far you've come,
And know you're on your way.

Forget about the past, and live for today!
Live your life with love and laughter,
Feel the joy in your soul,
And be sure to spread this message
To heal the world – mind, body and soul!

– With Love & Gratitude,
Lauretta Ryan, RMT Nova Scotia,
Registered Massage Therapist,
Reiki Master/Teacher

Angels by Your Side

Angels by our side
Staying with us all the way
Never leaving us, night or day.

Angels all around us
For each of us to feel
Loving us forever,
Knowing we are not alone.

Reach out to your angels
As they are always reaching out to you
Connect with your angels
For they want to be with you.

Your angels are full of love and grace
And they see you in this light
Always by your side
Always guiding you.

Just reach out to your Angels today!

– Karen Forrest, Words of Wisdom Counselling

From C-7 Rifle to Sword of Light: Karen's Journey

My journey from carrying a C-7 rifle in the military to my spiritual work carrying a sword of light has been an amazing journey of faith in following my life path. Through my military training, I quickly learned to handle the C-7 rifle for personal defence. Upon my retirement from the military in 2007, I readily exchanged my rifle for a symbolic sword of light. I have warrior energy, so it's no surprise that I joined the military and now no surprise that I carry a sword of light, as carried by Archangel Michael. This divine sword brightens my path and removes barriers of fear preventing me from moving forward on my life's journey.

I grew up in a military environment. My father served in the navy as a stoker (mechanical engineer) and then as a Military Policeman, and my grandfather served in the army during World War II. Every four years my father was posted to a new location. Then I joined the military and moved every four years. I have been from one end of Canada to the other and feel blessed to have experienced the beauty Canada has to offer.

I was born in Halifax, Nova Scotia, and no matter

where I lived in Canada, I always considered Nova Scotia to be my home. With my father's military postings I also lived in Ottawa, Ontario; Greenwood, Nova Scotia; and Winnipeg, Manitoba.

I have a very close-knit family. I grew up in a loving home that as a child I did not appreciate nearly enough. As an adult, I appreciate my mother's home-baked cookies and my father taking us kids and our friends to the park. I couldn't imagine my life without my older sister, Rhonda, younger sister, Lesa, and younger brother, Kevin. Rhonda and I were both born in the same year, so I literally cannot remember my life without Rhonda being there for me. I have fond memories of guarding over Lesa and her friends at school and today Lesa and I enjoy travelling together. Kevin is the baby of the family, although he might not appreciate being referred to as such, but in my heart he will always be my baby brother whom I am very proud of.

I was raised as a Roman Catholic, although I no longer associate myself with a particular religion as my focus is spirituality. I have childhood memories of reciting the rosary and attending weekly mass. My parents and maternal grandmother taught, and more importantly demonstrated, the true meaning of faith. I have always believed in God and angels, but in recent years I learned to go from believing to experiencing them.

I have always felt close to God, but didn't know how to connect with Him directly for guidance. I prayed to God, but that was about it. I believed angels were out there somewhere, but didn't realize they are truly by my side. As an adult, I remember my parents gifting me with a book about angel stories one Christmas. I loved the inspirational stories, but had no idea I would one day write my own book of angel stories.

In 1989, at age twenty-two, I joined the Canadian Armed Forces to escape minimum-wage dead-end jobs and to receive career training. I began my career as a private, working in communications as this was the fastest way in at the time. Four years later, I was involved in a serious car accident that changed my life. I hit black ice on the highway, lost control of my car and hit a semi-trailer truck. It was a miracle I survived this accident for I totalled my brand new Ford Mustang, where the air bags deployed upon impact.

I knew there was a reason I lived and consequently examined the direction my life was going. I sat down one night and asked God and my guardian angels to help me remain on my life path and give me the courage to make any needed changes in my life. I wanted to remain in the military, as I loved the adventure and serving my country, but I remembered my dream of becoming a nurse. Intuitively I realized I was a healer and a leader. I was now ready to pursue this dream. So I applied, and was consequently accepted, for a Bachelor of Nursing at the University of Calgary, with military sponsorship.

Thus started my path as a healer. Just one short year after graduating with my Bachelor of Nursing, I specialized as a Mental Health Nursing Officer. When I first joined the military, I had no idea that there were military mental health nurses. I remember my supervisor asking me if I would be interested in specializing in critical care nursing. I was standing in the hallway, replying no, that bored me, but I loved mental health. By coincidence, or more apt divine intervention, my commanding officer just happened to walk by at that precise moment. When she overheard my interest in mental health, she immediately stopped and asked if I would be interested in taking the next Advanced Mental Health Nursing Course in Calgary. Yet another step down my life's path.

The first time I literally felt an angel's presence was during a thirteen-kilometre rucksack march as part of my officer's training in Chilliwack, British Columbia. I have fairly good endurance, but it's strained when I am doing a forced march, wearing combat boots, carrying a fifty-pound rucksack, with a C-7 rifle slung over my shoulder. Passing this march was a must to proceed with my officer training to become a nurse. By the last few kilometres I was struggling to keep up the pace and my fifty-pound rucksack was feeling more like five hundred pounds. I remember praying to God and the angels, "Please help me finish this rucksack march on time. If I don't pass this, then I cannot proceed with my military nursing training. I know, God, I am meant to be a military nurse so for heaven's sake help me now."

Often when someone is falling behind, another soldier will encourage you forward – even literally push you forward if needed. But I didn't want anyone talking to me as I find this annoying when I simply want to focus on literally moving ahead one step at a time. And I certainly didn't want someone pushing me from behind so hard that I risked falling on my face. Within a minute of my prayer, I felt a soft pressure on my back, aiding me in moving forward but without being too pushy. Thankfully, this person didn't talk to me as I really needed peace and quiet to mentally focus on the rucksack march. I was so grateful for this person just simply gently being there for me. I was so tired and so focused that I did not take the time to look around to see who was helping me out. I simply thanked them for walking steadfastly behind me. Finally, I finished the march. What a relief. I turned around to again thank the person who helped me the last few kilometres. There was no one there! I instantly knew, without a doubt, it was my guardian angel that was by my side.

I am proud of my military nursing career and have never regretted joining the military. Highlights included my United Nations tour to Israel, working in communications in 1992 and deploying as a mental health nurse to Bosnia in 2002. As corny as it may sound, I felt honoured to have served my country and fellow military members. However, in 2004, as I began to focus on my spirituality even further,

I realized that it was soon time for me to retire from the military. It was time to move on with the next phase of my life path as a healer. I was medically released from the military in 2006, ready to begin focusing on my spiritual healing.

In 2004, while serving in Petawawa, Ontario, I attended, out of curiosity and a basic belief in angels, a workshop called "Learn to Talk to Your Angels." This was the beginning of my work as a spiritual healer. I was absolutely fascinated that you could connect directly with your angels and God and wanted to learn even more. I knew within my heart that I needed to take my spiritual training to the next level. I was unexpectedly drawn to angel healing, even though at first it sounded rather flaky, considering I came from a medical model. But once again, I honoured my life path and its unexpected turns.

As a spiritual healer, I desired credibility behind my name; therefore, I attended Doreen Virtue's Angel Therapy Practitioner Course® (2004) in California, which certified me as an Angel Therapy Practitioner®. Doreen is world-renowned for her angel work and I had read and respected her teachings on communicating with angels and the Divine. In November 2004, I was divinely guided to establish my private practice, Words of Wisdom Counselling. Later I extended my training with my Medium Mentorship Course (2005) and Professional Spiritual Teachers Program (2006), both taught by Doreen Virtue. I continue to attend numerous spiritual workshops and conferences and to read various spiritual books. As you can guess, I am an avid learner and reader. Bookstores are my favourite hangout. However, with all my learning, I remember to live what I believe in. I truly walk my talk.

When I was preparing to retire from the military, I certainly questioned God and my guardian angels if I should really give up nursing and focus on my spiritual work full-time. I was being head-hunted by hospitals to work as a mental health nurse, but I intuitively knew this was no longer my path as a healer. Working with angelic/divine healing had proven to be more effective and quicker than my traditional nursing healing.

I also asked myself, "What would it be like for me not to continue with offering angel readings and teaching angel workshops?" I cried at the thought of no longer doing my angel work. That was my answer straight from my heart. It was with a great leap of faith and tremendous courage that I finally decided to pursue my spiritual work full-time. This is a decision I have never regretted. I truly wanted to honour my life purpose, which meant continuing my journey as a spiritual healer.

As a result of my spiritual/angel training, I shifted from believing in angels to experiencing angels on a daily basis. My life is more peaceful and joyful as I continuously invoke angels/God to help me in all ways. Feeling at peace more often than feeling worried works for me.

I hold an inspiring vision where you connect directly with your angels and God and to know within your heart that your loved ones are at peace and continue to live on in the afterlife. I envision that all people can know and follow their own unique life purpose. My mission is to provide you with loving, guiding messages from your angels/ God and deceased loved ones in a peaceful atmosphere of confidentiality, comfort and divine light. I assist you in personally connecting with your angels and teach you how to receive angelic guidance in an atmosphere of respect and spiritual enlightenment. My private sessions and workshops support your personal healing, spiritual growth and understanding and help guide you in following your own life purpose.

My spiritual work is extremely rewarding as I have the pleasure of meeting beautiful, kind-hearted people with loving spirits here to make this world a better place. I love hanging out with loving, positive people. The most rewarding aspect of my work is observing how my clients' lives improve for the better so quickly once they call upon angelic/divine intervention. I know I make a tremendous positive difference in others' lives. People become more peaceful, relaxed, carefree, and lead even more meaningful lives as they release their fears and honour their life purpose. There is nothing difficult about my job as long as I practise what I preach and release any of my own limiting beliefs and surrender my fears. However, there are times I am saddened when I see people purposely choosing to live in fear or holding onto anger or unforgiveness because this depresses our spirit. How can you possibly experience peace and joy if you're enveloped in fear, anger and/or unforgiveness?

I decided to retire from nursing for two reasons. One, I was divinely guided to work full-time as an Angel Therapy Practitioner®/spiritual healer. Two, from experience I noticed how much more effectively, quickly, lovingly and gently angel/divine healing works compared to the traditional medical model. Why is spiritual healing more effective? It is divinely directed. God and the angels are healing you directly. Having said this, I realize there are times people need to choose and seek medical advice. You can incorporate angel/divine healing into your life along with medical care. No matter what method of healing you choose, always listen to your own intuition about what you need for that particular concern in your life. Your health is your responsibility. I encourage you to take control of your spiritual/mental and physical health. It is your life.

I love working with guardian angels, angels, Archangels, God and the ascended masters. There is a whole team of divine helpers by your side. Specifically, I always have Archangel Raphael, the healer, and Archangel Michael, the protector, by my side. I am in constant connection with my guardian angels and God. Remember, God is within you. You are never separate from the divine.

I was once asked how the world would be different if we all believed in angels and were willing to look to them for guidance. I am not here to convince everyone to believe in angels or to believe in God. This would create intolerance to others' spiritual/religious beliefs and there is enough intolerance in this world without my creating more. My military tours in Israel and Bosnia clearly demonstrated the negative effects of intolerance. However, if everyone sought direct guidance from loving higher beings, whether this is God or angels or Buddha or Jesus or whoever you believe in, and if we took the time to look deep within ourselves, then countries would be at peace and people would respect each other even if they held different values or religious or spiritual beliefs.

If you want to create more peace in this world, then live in peace yourself, heal yourself and respect other people's right to be different from you. This is why I strive to come from a peaceful and loving heart. I don't expect perfection from myself, but if I can live in peace more often than fear, worry, anger and intolerance, then I am making a greater difference in this world. And if I can help others achieve inner peace and love, then I know I've done my part in contributing to peace.

My contributions to a more harmonious world began with my military work as a peacekeeper. Now, my part in creating a more peaceful planet is through healing others and teaching people to lead a peaceful life.

Frequently Asked Questions

Question: Do I have angels around me?

Yes. Everyone does, even you. However, it is our choice if we desire to reach out to the angels or not. Everyone has a minimum of two guardian angels, one ministering and one teaching, which are with you from the day you are born to the day you die. Your guardian angels are constantly by your side, twenty-four hours a day, every day of the year. They never leave your side. It is with your guardian angels that I communicate most frequently in my private sessions.

Question: Do angels truly desire to communicate with me?

Absolutely. Your angels only desire to lovingly connect with you and assist you in your everyday life. As much as you wish to communicate with them, your angels desire even more to communicate with you.

Question: How can I become closer to my guardian angels?

By inviting them into your life. Ask to feel your angels' presence. During meditation hold the intent of connecting with your guardian angels. Just sit quietly in their presence so that you can become attuned to their magnificent energy, feel and presence.

Question: What do angels really look like?

Angels can appear in different ways. I often see them as beautiful coloured circles of light. Your guardian angels always appear to me standing beside your right shoulder, smiling, dressed in long, white gowns. You can also see angels as you expect them to look like with wings and gowns.

Question: Why can't I see angels?

To visually see angels is a clairvoyant capability. Not everyone is primarily clairvoyant. So please don't pressure yourself into "seeing" angels. You may simply "see" an angel by noticing an angel statue or unexpectedly seeing an angel painting or picture. Some people see them as coloured lights or white lights.

Question: How do people receive messages from angels or God?

There are four main ways to receive divine messages:

Clairvoyance: through visions, dreams, seeing images in your mind

Clairsentience: feeling in your body, gut instinct, smells. Most people are clairsentient so pay attention to what your body tells you.

Clairaudience: hearing angels, hearing words inside your head, as though you are talking to yourself, or outside your head

Claircognizance: a sense of knowingness. You know something but don't know how you know it. You just know it.

Question: Isn't it selfish for me to ask the angels for small things?

No, it is definitely not selfish. Your angels truly want to assist you in your life in all ways. Angels do not differentiate or label your requests as big or small; that is what humans do. They treat all of your requests in the same devoted manner, whether you are asking an angel to turn a traffic light green or asking for major healing. You simply need to ask.

Question: How do I ask my angels for help?

Seeking divine guidance from your angels is very easy. The most important aspect is holding the intent. You can say, pray, think or write to your angels. There is no wrong way to communicate with them. As soon as you begin to ask, your angels are instantly by your side, lovingly guiding you.

Question: How can I be certain I am really speaking to an angel?

If you are holding the intent of connecting with angels, then you will. When connecting with your angels, you will feel peaceful, calm, relaxed and protected. Angel messages ring true to you. When connecting to your ego, your lower self, you feel negative, down, or "off." It just doesn't feel right and does not ring true to you. Angels always communicate in a loving, supportive and positive manner. Your ego communicates in an indecisive, negative, put-down manner.

Question: Can I send angels to other people?

Yes, please do! What happens when you send extra angels to other people is that the angels will go to the higher being, the true part of yourself connected to the Divine of these people, and ask if they are willing to receive their angelic help. Their highest being will either accept or decline. In my experience, the vast majority of people appreciatively accept the angels' loving help.

Question: What if I can't remember which specific type of angel or archangel to call upon? Does it have to be a specific type or name of angel?

The angels are never concerned what name you call them or what specific type of angel you invoke. Although I may invoke guardian angels, including by specific name various archangels or other specific angels – for example, romance angels or angels of peace – you just simply need to hold the intent on connecting to angels and/or God. An angel would never say, "You called upon the wrong angel for what you need, so I won't help you." That's just not how it works. So talk to who you feel comfortable with in the spiritual world, whether that is guardian angels, archangels, angels, God, Jesus or whoever you associate with from your spiritual or religious beliefs.

Question: What angels do you see around me?

This varies from person to person, but you definitely have a group of angels around you. Along with your guardian angels, I see or hear other angels depending on your life purpose. For instance, if your life purpose involves bringing peace into this world, then I usually see angels of peace around you. I also see or hear your various angels depending on what you have asked the angels for help with – parenting angels for parents seeking to improve their relationship with their child or angels of romance for those seeking a soulmate relationship. Other common types of angels I connect with are angels of protection, angels of music, angels of creativity, angels of abundance, Archangel Michael, and Archangel Raphael or the healing angel.

Question: Do I have deceased relatives around me?

Yes. Everyone does, including relatives you may never have met, such as your deceased grandmother who died before you were born. You also have your deceased friends around you.

Question: Do our deceased relatives know what is going on in our lives since they died?

Very much so, as spiritually they are still a part of you and your life. So yes, your deceased grandmother is aware of her newest great-grandchild that was born. Your deceased relatives often tell me how they are in spirit at joyous family events such as weddings, graduations, baptisms and other special events.

Question: What are the most common messages that deceased people give you, as a medium?

Over and over again, your deceased loved ones reassure you that they are okay, at peace and send their love to you.

Question: Are my pets in heaven too?

Yes. Like us, our pets have souls that evolve in the afterlife. I sometimes have clients who are more interested in receiving messages from a beloved deceased pet than a deceased relative.

Question: As a medium, do you have dead people talking to you all the time?

Thankfully not anymore! When I first started receiving messages from dead people they would talk to me more frequently than I cared for as they knew I could hear them. For instance, I would be on the city bus going to work and suddenly the deceased mother of the stranger sitting next to me would start talking to me, wanting me to relay a message to her son. However, there was no way I was going to tell this stranger that his dead mother was talking to me! It would make me look like I'm nuts! However, once I became trained as a professional medium, I learned to control this. Archangel Michael acts as my bouncer and dead people can only talk to me when I give them permission to come through during my private sessions with my clients.

Question: Why are you are gifted in speaking to angels but I am not? How come some people are so intuitive and others are not?

We are all able to connect with angels and we are all psychic/intuitive. Some of us just need to relearn and rediscover our personal intuitive/psychic abilities and gifts. It's not that I am so "special" or "gifted." I did not see or hear dead people or angels as a child. I was not born a third-generation psychic. Far from it, my mother actually attends my workshops. I say this so you can understand that you too can rediscover your inherent intuitive abilities just like I did. This is why I offer so many workshops aimed at the normal, everyday, average person.

Question: So I can really learn to connect and communicate with angels too?

Yes, we all can.

Question: What made you become interested in your angel work when your background is military, mental health nursing?

I have always believed in angels and God, but did not know how to invoke them to help me in my everyday life. In 2004, by fluke – or so I thought – I attended a workshop called Learn to Talk to Your Angels. I thought I would check this workshop out and hoped it was not some weird, religious cult trying to suck me in. It turned out to be a spiritual workshop truly teaching me the basics of connecting with the angels. I was so fascinated I continued my spiritual journey by reading spiritual books and completing professional spiritual training, including my Angel Therapy Practitioner® course, Medium Mentorship Course and Professional Teachers Training Program – all certified by Doreen Virtue Ph.D. If you had asked me even five years ago if I would be working full-time as an Angel Therapy Practitioner®, talking to angels and dead people, I would have looked at you as though you were crazy.

Question: How do non-believers react to you?

They blink their eyes, cannot relate and ask no further questions about my work.

Question: How is a session over the phone different from a session in person?

There truly is no difference as I am working with energy and telepathic messages. You do not need to be in front of me to receive messages from your angels and facilitate angel healing. Most of my private sessions are over the telephone.

Question: Because you feel and hear people's angels during private sessions, are these interactions hard on you, on your body? Does it make you tired?

Communicating with your angels is not hard on me physically or mentally as I am trained in what I do. I know how to spiritually protect myself from being drained by my work. I certainly need to care for myself, which includes eating a vegetarian diet, meditating, exercising, chakra clearing (clearing energy centres within your body), etheric cord-cutting (releasing fear-based attachments within relationships) and balancing my life with fun and work. I rarely feel tired from my work, but I have learned my limits. It is actually energizing connecting with the higher vibrations of angels and God.

Question: Does your work ever become a burden to you?

I am passionate about my work, so it is never a burden, but I do take the responsibility associated with my work seriously.

Question: Do you have many follow-up clients?

Most of my clients follow up with me at some time or other. If they have had a private session, then they often choose to attend one or more workshops or vice versa. Many have subsequent appointments to continue healing. Other times when they need further angelic guidance, they seek follow-up appointments. Also, my clients may choose a separate session to receive messages from a deceased loved one or a deceased pet. Follow-up sessions vary with each client. However, I do not encourage clients to call me every day seeking guidance. This is why I offer workshops, so my clients can learn to seek divine/angelic guidance for themselves.

Question: What do you love most about your angel work?

Knowing that through angel messages and divine healing, my clients are incredibly healthier, happier and more peaceful. It doesn't get any better than that!

Glossary of Terms

As many people have different definitions for spiritual terms, I offer this glossary so that you may understand what I mean by each term.

Angels: Loving beings of Divine light, here to guide you towards your life purpose and assist you in every area of your life. Angels are messengers of God. They have never been human, so they only know feelings of love, joy and peace. Everyone has angels around them. Your angels love you unconditionally.

Archangels: Very powerful, loving angels who oversee the guardian angels. Common archangels are Archangel Michael (courage, protection, life purpose); Archangel Raphael (healing angel); Archangel Gabriel (messenger of God, assists parents, works with communication). Each archangel has specific roles. Please note that although the archangels have specific roles, you do not need to try and remember which archangel works with what role. You simply need to ask the archangels/God for help and they are instantly by your side. Various religions believe in various archangels; however, regardless of your religious affiliation the archangels help everyone who asks for their assistance. Foremost, archangels are spiritual, divine beings.

Ascended Masters: A great spiritual teacher or healer who once lived on this earth plane and continues to provide pure, loving guidance from the afterlife. Many are associated with major religions (Mother Mary, Jesus, Buddha, Mohammed), come from various cultures and are nondenominational.

Deceased Loved Ones: Our relatives/friends who have died and crossed over (gone to heaven, afterlife). Our deceased loved ones can still watch over us from beyond.

Fairies: Nature's angels. Fairies protect/heal the earth, animals and our pets.

God: A higher being, going by many different names: God, the Creator, the Source, the Divine. God loves you unconditionally and is always by your side.

Guardian Angels: Every person is born with at least two guardian angels that are with them from the day they are born until the day they die. Your guardian angels love you unconditionally and are always by your side waiting for you to ask for their help.

Medium: Someone with the ability to communicate with dead people.

Afterword

I wish to thank each and every person who contributed a story for this book. In sharing your stories you are helping others understand that they have angels and their deceased loved ones by their side. I shall continue writing more Angel story books. If you have any stories you would like to submit, please e-mail me: karen@karenforrest.com or call me: (902) 404-3103. My website can be found at: www.karenforrest.com. I look forward to hearing your treasury of personal stories.

May you always know and remember that you have loving angels constantly by your side, just waiting for you to reach out and ask for their help. You are not alone in this world. Since learning to ask for my angels' help, my life is so much easier, smoother and more peaceful.

I wish you peace within your heart. I send you love and light in your life in all ways. Never forget to connect with your angels today!

In love and light,
Karen Forrest
Words of Wisdom Counselling

About the Author

Karen is a truly gifted motivational speaker, spiritual counsellor and Angel Therapy Practitioner® and medium who counsels and teaches from a heart of compassion. She is very passionate about her healing work.

Always believing in angels, but not knowing how to connect with them, Karen became an Angel Therapy Practitioner® in 2004, certified by world-renowned Doreen Virtue Ph.D. Karen mastered an intensive Medium Mentorship Program (2005) and the Professional Spiritual Teachers Program (2006), both certified by Doreen Virtue Ph.D. Karen attended a Basic Mediumship Course by James Van Praagh in 2007.

Karen achieved a Bachelor of Nursing degree from University of Calgary and a diploma in Advanced Studies Mental Health Nursing from Mount Royal College, Calgary. To expand her knowledge in complementary therapies, Karen became a Reiki practitioner in 1996. Captain Karen Forrest (retired) honourably served seventeen years in the Canadian Armed Forces, retiring as a Mental Health Nursing Officer in 2006.

Karen, with guidance and encouragement from her Guardian Angels, commenced her Words of Wisdom Counselling practice in November 2004. Karen offers private angel readings and medium sessions. She is passing on her knowledge through various Angel workshops and lectures. Karen's life purpose involves connecting people with their Angels, God and deceased loved ones. It is a life purpose she takes to heart and pursues with absolute passion and a great leap of faith!

Karen can be contacted at www.karenforrest.com and (902) 404-3103.